THE QUEST FOR IDENTITY

FROM MINORITY GROUPS TO GENERATION XERS

Donald M. Taylor

PRAEGER

Westport, Connecticut
London

Library of Congress Cataloging-in-Publication Data

Taylor, Donald M.
   The quest for identity : from minority groups to Generation Xers / Donald M. Taylor.
      p.   cm.
   Includes bibliographical references and index.
   ISBN 0–275–97309–3 (alk. paper)—ISBN 0–275–97310–7 (pbk. : alk. paper)
   1. Group identity.   2. Identity (Psychology).   3. Ethnicity.   I. Title.
   HM753.T39   2002
   302.4—dc21   2002022440

British Library Cataloguing in Publication Data is available.

Library of Congress Catalog Card Number: 2002022440
ISBN: 0–275–97309–3 (hc)
      0–275–97310– 7 (pbk)

First published in 2002

Praeger Publishers, 88 Post Road West, Westport, CT 06881
An imprint of Greenwood Publishing Group, Inc.
www.praeger.com

Printed in the United States of America

The paper used in this book complies with the
Permanent Paper Standard issued by the National
Information Standards Organization (Z39.48–1984).

10 9 8 7 6 5 4 3 2 1

This book is dedicated to
My dad,
William M. Taylor.
His spirit lives in this book.

Contents

Preface

I am a privileged, White, male, academic, experimental social psychologist but the focus of this book is society's most disadvantaged. That is but one of the many contradictions that need to be acknowledged in order to understand the unique form this book has taken.

To begin with, despite the enviable quality of life enjoyed by many in society, and while recognizing many of the egalitarian advances that society has made in the last decades, I firmly believe that the gap between advantaged and disadvantaged is growing. Specifically, I believe we have carefully shielded ourselves from the desperate plight of our Aboriginal people, the majority of those in the African American community and the growing number of homeless youth. This book is about disadvantage in the context of plenty.

I have always preached to my undergraduate and graduate students that addressing social problems requires both head and heart. It is not enough to want to address a social issue with empathy and sympathy. Equally, you need to approach a social issue with a tough intellect. In this book I occasionally wear my heart on my sleeve, but you will also find I have presented a formal theory of disadvantage.

Experimental social psychologists conduct research in the laboratory and publish their results in journals that set the highest standards for objectivity. I am committed to this process and have always respected those norms in my writing. But I do research in disadvantaged communities, where I have gained as much insight through the privilege of personal encounters as I have from the scientific data I collect. And so in this book, I break the usual norms and share the personal experiences as well as the hard data.

Field research in the communities that are the focus of this book is an emotional roller coaster. Discouragement is a constant. Arduous, some would say dangerous, travel to remote communities in the harshest environment on earth pales with the direct, ongoing confrontation with the painful social problems that plague those who are disadvantaged and the lack of any obvious quick fix. Guilt is a constant companion. There is, of course, being constantly confronted with the fact that by dumb luck you were born into privilege, and no matter how much time you spend in disadvantaged communities, at the end of the day you escape to a world of relative affluence. The guilt is exacerbated by my own theorizing which places the source of disadvantage squarely in the hands of the power of my own cultural group. But discouragement and guilt are more than offset by an over-riding feeling of pure joy. The opportunity to witness the tundra in mid-winter and the all-enveloping heat of the inner city are spectacular enough. But to share relationships with the people who become life-long friends is the ultimate experience and overshadows everything else.

Even my acknowledgments are a contradiction. On the one hand I am blessed to learn from a group of colleagues and graduate students at McGill University while at the other colleagues and friends in disadvantaged communities openly welcome and enlighten me. I am truly privileged.

Finally, there is the contradiction of having me pretend to speak for those whose life experience is so different. I was excusing myself for this contradiction at a community meeting in a remote Arctic village when a respected elder rose and said, "Put a voice to our pain."

This book is my humble voice.

CHAPTER 1

Collective Identities in Crisis

There are groups in society that experience profound social problems and others that show signs of a growing social malaise. The problems include massive academic underachievement, family dysfunction, substance misuse, violence, and delinquent behavior. This highly unflattering profile applies to Aboriginal people, African Americans, and certain Hispanic groups. To this list I would add the ever-growing number of so-called "street kids" that roam our inner-city streets. Finally, to a lesser but no less frightening extent, I would even add those who have traditionally symbolized society's most privileged group, young White men. These are not the only groups who stand out as noticeably disadvantaged, but they are certainly among the most visible, and they happen to be the groups with whom I have had personal experience. The purpose of this book, as presumptuous as it may sound, is to acknowledge the reality that these groups are confronting, to understand that reality, and, through understanding, to seek a possible solution.

My professional role as an academic, involved in teaching and research, allows me the privilege of direct contact with these groups in their own communities in countries like Canada, the United States, South Africa, and Indonesia. I also happen to live in a country, Canada, where the quality of life is the envy of the world, which only serves to magnify the contrast with society's most disadvantaged.

It is no doubt this contrast, a contrast between my cozy academic tower in a privileged nation and the grim realities of the disadvantaged, that makes me lose my scientific detachment and feel emotionally spent every time I visit these communities. And so, I find myself writing this book in anger. No, not anger, for anger presupposes a target for my feelings, and I do not quite know who to blame. My inclination would be to target privileged, mainstream White men and, in particular, political, social, and educational leaders. But that would be too simple.

Blame does seem easy to pinpoint when we contemplate some of the world's more infamous genocides. The Holocaust, the killing fields of Cambodia, and the more recent Rwandan tragedy leave no doubt in anyone's mind about the purely evil intentions of the perpetrators. But what of apartheid in South Africa? Apartheid, which blatantly separated Black from White, was a policy that was universally condemned and made South Africa a pariah among nations, until the government's fall in 1994. The intention of the privileged White minority seemed all too clear. However, when apartheid proponents put their "spin" on the policy, it sounds frighteningly like what today are judged to be enlightened policies that celebrate cultural diversity and multiculturalism. That is, in countries like the United States and Canada, the notion that cultural minorities should be forced to assimilate to mainstream culture is deemed discriminatory. The current climate of cultural relativism espouses the view that cultural minorities should have their cultures respected. Thus, groups are encouraged to retain their cultural heritage and this may include members of a group living together in order to provide mutual support for their own culture while providing a defense against the ravages of assimilation. Proponents of apartheid in South Africa made precisely this argument. Different ethnic groups were segregated, they argued, not to prevent them from participation in the economic and political life of South Africa or to make them a target for blatant discrimination, but rather to allow their cultural identity to flourish. What was the intention of apartheid? It would appear from any vantage point to be intentionally discriminatory, but there is just enough rhetoric that is consistent with modern cultural relativism to convince some people that proponents of apartheid were well intentioned.

And finally, what of the systematic destruction of Aboriginal peoples in North America? The widespread rape and abuse of children who were forced to leave their communities to attend European-style schools aside, questions of intention are more complex. Missionaries probably thought they were doing Aboriginal peoples a great service by coercing them into Christianity. The deadly germs brought by Europeans, for which Aboriginal people had no immunity, were surely an unintended development.

Merchants are especially interesting. Yes, they traded their cheap "baubles" for expensive furs. And yes, they traded rifles for furs, one rifle for a pile of furs that stood from the rifle butt to its menacing tip. And yes, they made rifles longer and longer for the mere purpose of cheating Aboriginal peoples out of more furs. But do not merchants take advantage of you and me if the opportunity presents itself? The prices of entrées at my favorite ethnic restaurant are lower on the ethnic-language menu as compared with the English version of the menu. Are you telling me that the car salesman does not see me coming? So, I am guessing that merchants in the New World operated on the age-old principle of "Get as much as you can for as little as you can."

It is always easy to judge the intentions of those from a bygone era, when circumstances were different. If I had been raised at the turn of the century in the Deep South or had been an early pioneer in the New World, how would I have understood my own behavior? Obvious atrocities aside, I do not think I am in any position to judge fairly the motives of others, nor would that be constructive.

Does that mean that we should forget the past and pretend it did not exist? The complexities of persistent disadvantage need to be analyzed, and a historical perspective must be integrated with an analysis of current reality. Such an exercise may require probing the prejudices of peoples past and present but only to serve the goal of, first and foremost, finding closure for the emotional scars of society's most disadvantaged and, second, of genuinely understanding today's grim reality.

In the final analysis, every case of profound disadvantage is rooted in a lack of understanding. How do you solve a problem if you do not genuinely understand the source of the problem? So what I really am is not angry but more frustrated at the persistence of severe disadvantage. Venting my frustration would be cathartic for me personally, I suppose, but it solves nothing. However, if I am correct, attempting to propose an explanation may be a constructive exercise. Even if I am proved wrong, at least I may stimulate others to address the issue.

AN AUTHOR'S INSECURITY

Authors typically do not begin a book by justifying their undertaking, but my insecurity, indeed defensiveness, about writing this book compels me to explain its intent and perspective. I feel no need to justify the topic. The desperate plight of society's most disadvantaged groups demands immediate attention. There are, however, two sources of my defensiveness. First, I am an academic social psychologist working in a research-oriented

department within a faculty of science. My career has involved writing scientific books and articles, and I have come to feel comfortable conforming
to the challenging norms of my discipline. I cannot escape the scientific
rigor of these norms, nor do I wish to, and yet I am certain that my theories,
observations, and conclusions will often stray from these norms. That is, in
the process of conducting research, scenarios arise and observations are
made that have no place in scientific discourse. But often these real-life personal encounters have a lasting impact and, in the course of scientific writing, I have often thought, "If only I could recount this anecdote, the point
would be clear." In the present volume, I finally get the opportunity to
share these personal experiences. Part of me wishes to apologize for such
transgressions, but in truth, I feel so compelled to share my personal observations that I will not take great pains to censor them. I only hope that they
do not detract from the formal theorizing, which, in the final analysis, is all I
have to offer in terms of genuine constructive change.

Speaking of scientific objectivity, there is already one bias that is bound
to color my analysis. It is a bias that confronts every experimental social
psychologist who supplements laboratory research with extensive work in
the field: you naturally develop a liking and respect for the individuals you
come to know and that includes the culture they represent. My experiences
in Aboriginal communities, in racially diverse disadvantaged urban centers, and in serving hot dogs to street kids from a van that tours the city in
the deep of night no doubt shape my theoretical orientation. I know they do
from the very fact that I feel reticent to even write about the devastating social problems these communities confront. I feel far more comfortable sharing the riches these communities have to offer. This is not to suggest that I
will shy away from confronting salient social problems. Nevertheless, my
positive bias is likely to unconsciously color my analysis.

The second source of my disquiet lies in the balance between right and
obligation when addressing the topic of this volume. I am a White male
who, despite spending a good deal of time in disadvantaged communities,
is pretending to have something to say about the experience of others.
Moreover, my ideas are no doubt partly shaped by members of disadvantaged groups who have directly and indirectly shared their experiences
and observations with me. Am I then speaking for them when their own
voice would be so much clearer? Do I even have the right to analyze the experience of other groups?

The dilemma about the right of a member of one culture to analyze another might, until recently, have been dismissed summarily. The notion
that only a member of a particular culture has the right to speak of, or for,
that culture seems on the surface to be patently absurd. Indeed, many of the

best observations of North American culture come from writers of a different culture, and the validity of their observations may arise precisely because they are one step removed from the culture they are observing.

But we have shifted dramatically from a resource-based economy to an information-based economy and that has made the issue of intellectual property a hotly debated subject. After all, if information is a valued resource, then the originator of the information must receive credit and retain some ownership of that information, be it a "hit" song, magazine article, or scientific breakthrough. Defining credit and ownership with respect to information is a difficult but serious business. I have heard more than one academic debate resolved by concluding that the first person to "write an idea down in any form" would be considered the owner of that intellectual property.

Culture is ultimately information that members of a culture, through prolonged commerce in and with that culture, carry around in their heads. As such, it is information that is a valued resource. Thus, the notion that only members of a culture can claim ownership of vital cultural information is not as absurd as it seems on the surface. Further, the power of the culture in question may be critical. It is common for the United States to provoke cultural comment because of its prominence and influence. Americans are used to being commented on by others and do not often feel culturally threatened in any profound way. But for less powerful cultures, the issue may be more delicate.

Two illustrations come to mind. The first involves a New York State university that was offering summer courses in minority languages and proudly announced that a linguist would be teaching an introductory course in an Aboriginal language. To the university's surprise, several chiefs of the language group in question insisted that the course not be offered. Their rationale was that the tribe would lose something the minute white mainstreamers could speak their language. It was as if their "code" would be broken.

The second example arose some six months after I had been living in the Philippines, where I must confess I had mastered only a few words of the national language, Tagalog. A visiting Caucasian North American scholar came to give a colloquium and, to my embarrassment, began the lecture in fluent Tagalog. I was feeling totally inadequate until, to my surprise and secret delight, my Filipino colleagues reacted negatively to the guest's use of their language. The revealing comment was "He was too fluent in Tagalog." The implication was that speaking in less than fluent Tagalog would have been a sign of respect, but complete fluency made people feel they had been robbed of something precious.

I have been privileged to learn firsthand from peoples in culturally different disadvantaged communities. By writing about their reality, am I robbing them of their identity, am I breaking their code? I do not know the answer to these questions except to feel a selfish need to share my observations in the faint hope that even if they are judged erroneous, they will have at least forced critics to confront the issues squarely. But I also know that I would feel equally distressed if I chose to remain silent. As that elder once said to me, "Please put a voice to our pain."

At a more pragmatic level, I wonder if by addressing the social problems confronting disadvantaged groups, I may only be making their problems more salient to themselves first and to society at large more generally. And perhaps those minority group members who have shared the most with me will themselves feel they have inadvertently, through me, contributed to the propagation of a negative image both within and outside their community.

I am confident about the constructive value of stimulating an awareness of social issues within the community, at least as far as the research process is concerned. On more than one occasion I have seen a community benefit from the research process, not so much the research per se, but the process. I well remember the trepidation I felt when launching a survey of language ability and usage in a remote Arctic village of some 1,000 inhabitants. The survey was prompted by a local Inuit committee that had questions about the appropriate language of instruction for their children in school. What gave rise to the question were the complexities confronting a small community where an indigenous language, in this case Innuttitut, was in competition with not one but two world languages, English and French. They were concerned that their language would be lost forever.

At a series of lengthy community meetings, where norms dictate that everyone must have a say, the research process proved highly constructive. In order to prepare our survey instrument, we as researchers needed to know what exactly the community meant by fluency in a language; and which contexts in the community were particularly diagnostic of language use and power. Our naïveté as scientists, coupled with our need for precision, prompted endless, highly fruitful discussions.

The result was a community that had defined the issues clearly for us as researchers and, equally importantly, for itself. Indeed, the community was so committed to the research that the social scientist's dream came true. In answer to the question, who should fill out the questionnaire, I hesitatingly responded that to be at all valid we would need a 10 percent sample, which meant a full 100 people. The immediate reply was, "But how will the voices of the other 900 residents be heard?" And so it happened that everyone over the age of 15 completed a questionnaire. Moreover, for those who were known to be out on the tundra hunting, skidoos were dispatched with questionnaires to make sure that everyone in the community contributed.

Never before, or since, have I been able to say that I obtained not a sample, but an entire population. But more important, the process had made the issue of language salient and its facets and implications more clearly understood. For example, the community clearly understood that the fate of its own language, Innuttitut, while apparently unassailable, was nonetheless under great threat. The survey results showed clearly that, among the young and in the formal job setting, the mainstream languages of English and French were replacing Innuttitut. The community became aware that its own language may well follow the fate of so many indigenous languages and become extinct. Thus, I am comfortable with the idea of raising issues in the community, especially because genuine community-based research springs from the needs of the community itself.

I worry more about raising awareness of a community's social problems outside the community, as in the case of the present volume. However, unwanted circumstances have conspired to provide me with an all too convenient escape from this dilemma. The fact is that the stereotypes of certain minorities are already so negative, and the social problems so pervasive, that raising awareness of them explicitly is not likely to alter existing stereotypes. Moreover, it will become clear that my theoretical perspective is one that holds all of us accountable and, in the final analysis, any one group's disadvantage diminishes us all. Perhaps in our shared diminished state, we may find a shared solution.

Scope of the Volume

At first glance, the focus of this volume is the academic underachievement experienced by large numbers of Aboriginal students. A cursory examination of the achievement levels of different groups in society reveals that Aboriginal groups are in the unenviable position of consistently occupying the lowest position, a level of underachievement that is so disparate from mainstream norms that Aboriginal children mature with little or no hope for themselves personally or their group as a whole.

But the present volume is about much more. First, while emphasis will be placed on formal education, the wider concern is with the familial, social, economic, political, and mental health of all those communities that are under siege. Education is a particularly important domain because it is a pervasive institution that impacts children as well as adults and because it is the institution that purports to prepare young people for the future by providing the economic, social, political, and moral resources needed to allow them to participate fully in society. However, the arguments I will apply to education hold equally true for occupational success and social adjustment. Indeed, Aboriginal communities suffer an array of social problems, including poor nutrition, family dysfunction, substance misuse, chronic underemployment, and poor mental health. Thus, while my emphasis will be on formal education, the wider concern is with adjustment in every important domain of life.

Second, academic underachievement is not an experience that is unique to Aboriginal people. It just happens to be a problem that is especially challenging for Aboriginal people. It also happens to be, not coincidentally, a social context that has occupied a large slice of my professional life. But academic underachievement is equally problematic for an array of inner-city minority groups in North America, including African Americans, Mexican Americans, and Puerto Ricans. Again, my personal experience with conducting research in inner-city contexts points strikingly to similarities with the experiences of Aboriginal people. The ideas expressed in this volume apply equally to all these groups.

I will also apply my analysis to a particularly challenging group, who in no sense qualify as a cultural or ethnic group in the usual sense. I am speaking here of street kids. It might seem on the surface that my only reason for including "street kids" is because I happen to conduct research and work with this particular group of young people. But it is my firm belief that the issues confronting society's ethnically disadvantaged apply equally to homeless youth, which warrants their alleviation. That is, one popular conception of street kids is that they are young people who have failed in, or have been rejected by, mainstream society and have, therefore, replaced mainstream culture with a subculture of their own, built largely around peer support. It is this folk theory that I question and that draws me to their plight. I will argue that they confront the same challenges as society's disadvantaged ethnic minority groups.

With some trepidation, I will even extend my analysis to include the growing underachievement and social malaise plaguing male students in mainstream North America. My purpose for including young mainstream men is not to suggest for one minute that their circumstances even remotely resemble those of society's most disadvantaged groups. Nor am I suggesting that young women, by inference, are privileged by comparison. The inclusion of young mainstream men is, first, because they show early signs of the profile of social problems that beleaguer disadvantaged groups. Second, and more important, I believe that the same processes, albeit on a very reduced scale, are beginning to impact on a group that until recently has been one of society's privileged groups.

In summary, the volume will emphasize the academic underachievement of Aboriginal people but will be extended to include the academic, economic, and social problems confronting a variety of societal groups including African Americans, Puerto Ricans, Mexican Americans, street kids, and young, White mainstream men. I hesitated before naming specific groups so early in this volume, fearing that minority readers might feel put under a microscope and mainstream readers might dismiss the volume as irrelevant to them. I can assure readers that no group will escape analysis and comment. I firmly believe that the profound psychological malaise that characterizes some communities can be found making its presence felt in society as a whole.

Theoretical Framework

The very first sentence in this chapter may well have raised the ire of many readers. Attributing any characteristic to an entire group, especially when the characteristics are not particularly socially desirable, is often viewed as odious from the point of view of liberal-thinking individualism. The argument is that the individual is the rightful focus of attention and that those who characterize entire groups are engaging in a form of discrimination.

The real question is whether group differences are real or imagined. The most eloquent case for not denying the reality of group-based differences has been made by Thomas Sowell, the noted political economist. Sowell (1983) is an African American scholar who sets out to address the delicate issue of African American–White group-based differences. Instead of basing his argument for the inescapable reality of group differences on racial groups, he begins with an analysis of two White groups, early Irish and German settlers to the East Coast of the United States. His argument is that, while Irish farmers were the first to arrive and therefore had access to the most arable lands, they did not perform well. Conversely, German farmers who came later, and were thus relegated to less desirable resources, nevertheless flourished through hard work and a long-term perspective.

Sowell's focus on differences between two White mainstream groups is inspired. Had he, as I might have, attempted to make the case for ethnic group-based differences directly, ideological barriers would have been triggered immediately. Mainstream readers would dismiss a focus on groups as politically incorrect, and no disadvantaged group reader wants to be reminded of group-based shortcomings. Sowell, by launching his claim with a comparison between two White mainstream groups, immediately takes the sting out of addressing questions about group-based differences.

Recognizing the reality of group-based differences, I have been glibly referring to a variety of different groups as if somehow each was a well-defined social unit. Of course, it would be a mistake to argue that social groups are homogeneous. Individual differences within any group are essential to ensure its very survival. Groups require a variety of roles to be fulfilled, and creative solutions to problems confronting the group are needed. Without the individual differences that allow for a diversity of skills, no group would survive. Moreover, for any specified dimension, the individuals within a group distribute themselves with respect to that dimension. Thus, for any particular dimension, groups are not so different that there is no overlap in the distribution of the individuals within the different groups.

This point has been made repeatedly with respect to the hotly debated issue of race and intelligence. Even when the average IQ score for one group is different from that of another, this does not mean that all members of one group have an IQ that is lower, or higher, than all members of the other group. It simply means that individual members of the two groups tend to be concentrated around different IQ scores. Clearly, there will be considerable overlap in the distributions so that many individual members of the lower group will in fact score higher than, perhaps, even the average for the group with the higher average.

So, when groups are judged to be different on a particular dimension, what is being suggested is that, while there may well be an overlap in the distributions of the individuals belonging to different groups, the concentration in the distribution of one group is different from the concentration in the other.

Acknowledging the reality of individual differences within groups, however, should not deflect us from deriving explanations that may be associated with the shared experiences of virtually all members of a group. The academic underachievement and social problems confronting severely disadvantaged groups is so pervasive that it compels the theorist to seek explanations at the group level. Indeed, if only a very few members of a particular group failed to achieve normal standards, there would be no social issue and certainly no theoretical or social link between achievement and group membership. The reality is, however, that despite clear examples of dramatic individual successes from every disadvantaged group, the vast majority are contributing in varying degrees to the statistics that paint such a demoralizing portrait of life for society's most disadvantaged groups.

Thus, in the present volume, I will be seeking explanations that revolve around the shared experience of group members. Any group's shared experience arises in the context of by comparison with, or because of other societal groups. My theory, then, will find its roots in intergroup relations. The aim will be to derive a theory at the intergroup level that will touch the psychological functioning of every severely disadvantaged group member.

The Psychology of Self

There is no more central psychological construct and process than the "self" and, thus, the psychology of "self" will form the basis of my theoretical analysis. Human beings stand out as unique in a variety of ways, including the capacity for sophisticated language and abstract thought, but more than anything, it is the human capacity to reflect on the self that makes us distinctive.

All human experience is processed through the self. Much that is automatic may be screened out at an earlier or more primitive level of processing, but at some point all experience, no matter how apparently trivial, was, or is, processed through the self. In this sense, the self is the pivotal human cognitive process that orients the individual toward meeting his or her needs.

The self is experienced at a very personal level. I feel profoundly that I am me across time and situations. Whether I am very much alone or acting in concert with members of my group, I experience my behavior as very much emanating from me. I view self, then, as a very personally experienced cognitive process arising out of our unique human capacity to reflect consciously on our own existence that orients the individual to meeting his or her needs.

Clearly, from my perspective, a healthy self is the minimum requirement for effective human functioning. Any individual, or group of individuals, who suffers less than a fully articulated self will be socially dysfunctional. My theory of self postulates that there are four key components to the self: personal identity, personal esteem, collective identity, and collective esteem.

The pivotal explanatory concept for my theory of self is collective identity. I will argue that what society's most disadvantaged groups suffer from is an unclear collective identity. The consequences of an unclear collective identity are, I will argue, catastrophic.

My concept of collective identity differs from similar concepts such as "self-concept" and "self-esteem" in two important ways. First, the focus of most notions of self is on the unique personal qualities of the individual. I will argue that identity involves both personal and collective elements and that the collective dimension of identity takes psychological precedence over personal identity.

Second, I will argue that too much attention has been paid to the "self-esteem" dimension of identity, with correspondingly less appreciation for the definitional, or "mental blueprint," dimension of identity. Quite simply then, my thesis is that the explanatory process involves problems with collective identity, not personal identity or self-esteem.

My theoretical challenge is to explain why communities come to be characterized by collective identities that are in crisis, which in turn lead inevitably to social dysfunction. Consistent with my intergroup perspective, it will be argued that groups who experience widespread academic underachievement and social problems confront a delicate balancing act involving competing collective identities. The specific collective identities at issue are cultural. All severely disadvantaged groups confront integrating "mainstream" collective identity or culture, on the one hand, and their "heritage" collective identity or culture, on the other. Those whose culture is represented by the dominant group in society can never fully appreciate just how momentous the juggling act must be for severely disadvantaged group members. The best I can do from my privileged position is reflect on minor personal incidents that offer at least some superficial insight into the profound challenge of confronting incompatible collective identities. My most vivid personal experience with such cultural discontinuity was more symbolic than real. I found myself in a small, crowded airport waiting for a twin-engine Otter plane to brave the minus-40-degree temperatures and driving snow in order to shepherd me from one tiny isolated Arctic community to the next village some 45 minutes away. I was feeling like a truly '90s kind of person, because slung over my shoulder, made enormous by a suitably thick parka, was a brand new laptop computer in its very own multipocketed carrying case. As I was about to confront the elements en route to the now awaiting plane, an Inuit lady handed me a 6-month-old child, complete with diapers and a tin of applesauce. Her only request was that I deliver the child to his, unknown to me, uncle in the next village. As I sat in my dilapidated seat surrounded by the fresh smell of old diesel fuel, I contemplated the discontinuity of cultures that would have me cradling a computer in one arm and trusted with someone's precious young child in the other. I could only imagine what it would be like to negotiate such disparate cultures on a daily basis, where the integration process was not symbolic but necessary for survival.

Beyond the enormity of resolving cultural discontinuity, I will argue that problems are exacerbated when there is a large power differential between the competing cultures. Power differentials of the magnitude referred to here include slavery and, more generally, colonialism. Theorizing that serious social dysfunction arises in groups that have been required to articulate an integrated collective identity in the context of colonialism is not novel. The present theory expands on current proposals by arguing that the integrated collective identity process is made virtually impossible because individual group members have no clearly identified schema for the competing collective identities or cultures they are required to integrate. That is, theories that emphasize the difficulties associated with integrating discontinuous cultures presume that there exist two clearly defined but incompatible cultures. What will be argued here is that severely disadvantaged groups do not have the benefit of either a clear schema for mainstream culture nor a clear vision of the heritage culture, let alone attempt a meaningful integration of the two. Valueless colonialism is the label I apply to this dual loss of clarity in collective identity.

Identity overload represents a second process that can disrupt collective identity. For severely disadvantaged groups, the lack of a clear cultural schema in the form of valueless colonialism is most disruptive to collective identity. Identity overload exacerbates the problem of collective identity for severely disadvantaged groups, but it is the primary source of disruption in collective identity for street kids and young mainstream men.

I will argue that a clearly defined collective identity arises where a culture provides its members with clear reference standards upon which to build a strong collective identity. When a society offers too many alternative standards, rather than providing the individual with choices, it serves to confuse and disorient the development of collective identity. I will argue, for example, that Aboriginal people in particular have been bombarded with social change so rapidly that assimilating the information into a collective identity is impossible. In the case of young mainstream men, I will argue that society offers so many diverse models in the domain of family, education, career, and lifestyle that collective identity is poorly articulated and collective demotivation is the inevitable result.

The four key stages to the present theory, then, involve "collective identity," "valueless colonialism", and "identity overload," which lead to "collective dysfunction." Briefly stated, it will be argued that severely disadvantaged groups are required to integrate two poorly defined cultures or collective identities, differing widely in power, into a coherent collective identity that can serve as a blueprint for living. The result of this impossible task is a shared state of demotivation that is characterized by alienation, lethargy, incoherent behavior, and a focus on the present, not the future.

Chapter Organization

I begin in Chapter 2 with an analysis of various social groups in society with a view to pinpointing which groups are especially prone to academic underachievement and social problems and which groups are consistently more successful. An attempt will be made to also specify the social conditions that appear to differentiate between the two group categories. In Chapter 3, we begin our explanatory quest by describing the pivotal concept of collective identity. This will require wrestling with the elusive challenge of defining "culture."

In Chapter 4, I will review current theories of cultural deficit and difference, with a view to describing their implications for collective identity. My own theory of valueless colonialism and its impact on collective identity will be outlined in Chapter 5. Identity overload is the theme for Chapter 6, and I will apply the concept to the recent rise in ethnic nationalism, political separation movements and the growing reality for young mainstream men.

In Chapter 7, the link between collective identity and collective demotivation will be outlined. Finally, Chapter 8 will attempt an integrated summary leading to specific interventions that may address the social problems confronting too many societal groups.

A Note on Style

Writing scientific articles requires referencing virtually every assertion that may form the building block of a theory or hypothesis (see *Publication Manual of the American Psychological Association*, 4th ed., 1995). The rationale for this norm of scientific writing is laudable: It ensures that credit is given to other scientists for providing the base information upon which your own theory and research is based. Furthermore, it lends credibility to your arguments.

While I concur totally with this rationale, the result in current scientific writing is referencing that is out of control. It has become almost impossible to follow a writer's argument because almost every sentence is interrupted with some bracketed reference citing previous research and theory. Moreover, the essential purpose for referencing is lost. Eighty percent of the references in a scientific article refer to research that is of little genuine consequence for the writer's argument. Rendered inconsequential in this process are the 20 percent of citations that were highly influential in the development of the scientist's argument and which deserve visible acknowledgment.

For these reasons, I will refrain from endless citations that serve to break up the flow of the text. Where I believe a major contributor to the arguments needs to be cited, I will do so. Obviously, these will be works that I believe to be influential in current thinking generally and in the development of my own arguments in particular.

CHAPTER 2

Society's Disadvantaged Groups: The Grim Reality

No society wants to be confronted with its own shortcomings. Criminals are hidden behind bars, the mentally ill are secluded in institutions, and the poor are congregated in places that keep them well out of sight. And when a city plans to attract many visitors, as in Atlanta on the eve of the Olympic games, it literally ensures the invisibility of the poor by physically moving them to a faraway corner of the city.

Similarly, there is a reluctance to acknowledge the reality of society's most disadvantaged groups: Out of sight, out of mind. Making it even more difficult to confront issues of inequality squarely is the emergence of a social ideology that mitigates against ongoing reality checks.

The ideology in question is cultural relativism, and it is as much a moral imperative as it is an all-embracing ideology. The current climate of cultural relativism, or cultural agnosticism (Sowell, 1983), dictates that groups be viewed as different and that these differences be celebrated. To be avoided are comparisons that imply that one culture may be "better" or "worse" than another. The rise of cultural relativism as a pervasive ideology is not surprising given that it represents a natural reaction to decades of explicit cultural ethnocentrism that preceded it. In an age of global communication, increased cultural diversity and the moral confrontation with the civil rights movement has made it more difficult to make a simple ethnic dichotomy between "good guys" (us) and "bad guys" (them). Blatant ethnocentrism has given way to a social norm that makes it politically incorrect to devalue any cultural group.

Although cultural relativism may be well intentioned, when taken to the extreme it may come to represent a form of cultural ethnocentrism. Sowell (1983) has criticized cultural relativism on factual grounds. He argues that the inescapable reality is that certain groups perform much better than others. Cynically he concludes that "much of the oppression in the world would not be possible if some groups did not have heavier firepower, more effective technology, or greater wealth, than others" (p. 136–37). Bloom (1987) is equally critical of cultural relativism but emphasizes the moral dimension. He cites the dramatic case of a culture that engages in genocide. Should such a culture be judged the moral equal to one that promotes equality?

My own confrontation with cultural relativism came while engaged in fieldwork in multiethnic urban centers in the United States. School authorities had great difficulty convincing parents from one particular group that they should allow their daughters to attend school and refrain from subjecting them to genital operations. A second group prided itself on being a "revenge" culture, and young males insisted that they be permitted to bring weapons to school. I discovered that my idealized and intellectually arrived at cultural relativism was instantly challenged at a "gut" level.

Having attacked the extremes of cultural relativism, it is important that its essence not be discarded and that we appreciate its complexities. Take the current debate over language in the United States. Cultural relativists point out that Spanish is equal to English in terms of its capacity to allow for the complete range of human communication. Opponents will agree with the relativist, but then continue with the observation that, because English is the dominant world language, Hispanic Americans need to forget their Spanish and assimilate to the English reality as quickly as possible. But the "superiority" of English is a structural one based on cultural power. If the structure were governed by relativism, then perhaps both languages would have equal status and both might become legitimate and necessary human resources.

These complexities arise when we turn our attention to the concept of relativism as it applies to the relationship of culture to academic achievement. Groups that do well academically, as defined by Western formal schooling, are not inherently "better" than cultural groups that perform less well. In this sense, cultural relativism is preserved. However, when the two groups share the same geographical space and for whatever reason academic success brings with it economic, social, and political advantages, then the differences do have profound evaluative overtones. To deny this reality means that respect for cultural differences is superficial and can only be interpreted as a form of cultural ethnocentrism because it legitimizes taking no steps to address the problem of academic underachievement and its attendant consequences.

Indeed, any form of superficial respect for cultural differences is ethnocentric. Encouraging Aboriginal people to retain their heritage culture seems, on the surface, to be an expression of cultural respect. However, heritage languages are not formally recognized in the world of business, education, the courts, or government. If respect were genuine, then heritage languages would have a status equal to that of majority languages. Without such status, the superficial expression of respect is nothing more than ethnocentrism, acknowledging in concrete terms that one language predominates over another.

SOCIETY'S MOST DISADVANTAGED

In North America, certain Hispanic groups, African Americans, and Aboriginal people consistently occupy the lowest rungs on the academic ladder. Aboriginal people, including Aboriginal Indian and Inuit in both Canada and the United States, consistently demonstrate the lowest levels of academic achievement among all recognized ethnocultural groups. The extent of the underachievement and associated social problems in Aboriginal communities and among African Americans needs to be documented so that any societal neglect of the problems under the guise of cultural relativism can be interpreted for what it is: a form of disguised cultural ethnocentrism, more precisely Eurocentrism.

In the following pages, two tables are presented, one focusing on Aboriginal people in Canada (Table 2.1), the other on African American, Hispanic, and Aboriginal poeple in the United Sates (Table 2.2). The tables do not represent an exhaustive analysis of every disadvantaged group. They are presented merely to indicate that the statistics underline that Aboriginal people and African Americans, among others, are severely disadvantaged. A cursory examination of their relative academic performance, economic conditions, and the prevalence of social problems makes any simple denial unthinkable, and denial is what prevents us from honestly addressing the issue.

Two points need to be made about the statistical profile. First, even the superficial statistics depict a bleak reality in terms of the academic, economic, social, and health-related reality for these disadvantaged groups. Second, and here I rely on personal experience, even these bleak statistics need to be questioned. There is little merit in presenting an optimistic

Table 2.1
Aboriginal People in Canada

	Aboriginal	Total Canadian
Education		
No formal schooling or less than grade 9	70%	32%
Some postsecondary education	55%	84%
Income & Employment		
Had income less than $2,000*	25%	15%
Over $40,000	5%	15%
Unemployed	24%	11%
Social Problems		
Mortality rate due to accidents & violence	32%	8%
Suicide rate (per 1,000)	34%	14%
Housing		
Average number of persons per dwelling	3.5	2.7
Receiving social assistance	29%	

*All currency in Canadian dollars.

Source: Statistics Canada (1991, 1986)

Table 2.2
White, African American, Hispanic, and Aboriginal People in the United States

	White	African American	Hispanic	Aboriginal
Education				
4 or more years of college	25.9%	15.5%	10.9%	9.4%
High school drop-out rate	9.8%	11.6%	25.0%	26.0%
Income and Employment				
Median income	$49,023*	$29,404	$29,608	$21,619
Persons below poverty level	10.5%	26.%1	25.6%	31.2%
Unemployment rate	3.1%	6.3%	5.6%	
Social Problems				
Female head of houshold, no spouse present	14.2%	45.1%	23.7%	26.2%
Teenage birth rate, per 1000	45.4%	85.3%	–	–
Delinquency rate per 1000 youth	51	124	–	–
Homicide rate–males per 100,000	6.7	47.1	–	–

*All currency in U.S. dollars.

Source: U.S. Census Bureau (2000).

analysis if it only serves to divert attention and responsibility away from the real issue.

One way the statistics can be misleading is the role played by school dropouts. On standardized tests, it is only those who are in school who take the test and thereby contribute to the school's overall performance. In disadvantaged communities, there are a disproportionate number of dropouts. If we presume that dropouts tend to be weaker students, then the test scores, which do not include dropouts, may be inflating the reality for young people in that community.

Dropouts are not the only source of misleading optimism about the academic performance of students from disadvantaged families. I am involved in an ongoing research project in an inner-city American metropolis that has pioneered a two-way bilingual program that runs from kindergarten through the eighth grade. An equal number of Hispanic and Anglo students are integrated into the same classroom, where half the instruction is in Spanish and the other half in English. Years of formal research, using standardized tests, have underscored the two-way benefits. Hispanic students maintain their Spanish and rapidly acquire fluency and literacy in English. Anglo students add Spanish proficiency to their English skills.

The suppressed statistics on the plight of minority students became evident recently when we sought an appropriate "control" group against which to compare the performance of our Hispanic students in the two-way program. We wanted a cadre of Hispanic students who were in the same school system but were in all-English classes, not our special bilingual classes. To our surprise, while there were large numbers of such students, none had been subjected to the standard tests that are used to generate statewide and national statistics. The reason these Hispanic students had not been tested did have some rational basis. In the drive for more accountability, school administrators are judged by the "bottom line," the performance of their students on standardized tests. Administrators of multiethnic schools pointed out that such a "bottom line" criterion was unfair because many of the students in culturally diverse schools are being tested on standard English tests when many of the students are new to the language. To address this inequity, newcomers to English are not permitted to be formally tested for a period of three years.

The result of this decision is that we have no "control" students, which is a minor inconvenience. Of greater significance is that, again, for reasons that are understandable, students who might be expected to perform poorly on standardized tests are not included in any formal comparison of ethnic groups. Thus, the disparity between ethnic groups may well be greater than published statistics indicate.

Furthermore, educators in severely disadvantaged schools wrestle with real dilemmas about academic standards on a daily basis. Do they maintain normal academic standards and have their students confront persistent failure, or do they set standards that are lower? By lowering the standards carefully, students can be challenged but experience some success. Over time, the standards can be slowly raised until they match those of mainstream students. The choice is not an easy one. Setting mainstream standards in an uncompromising manner ensures that the already high dropout rate will reach astronomical proportions. Lowering standards would seem to cheat students in terms of further advancement.

Consciously or unconsciously, standards are often lowered. For example, I have worked in schools where a child is deemed to have "attended" school no matter how late he or she arrive and how many classes he or she skips. I have witnessed countless classes where discipline and attendance issues were so pervasive that an entertaining movie takes the place of teaching. The point here is that the statistics, bleak as they are, may be misleading because they do not reflect how desperate the situation is.

Totally incongruous cultural discontinuities can exacerbate the problem. The classic one is the fact that the school year in Aboriginal communities looks very much like the schedule in mainstream urban schools. The year begins in September and ends in June. Of course, key Aboriginal cultural activities such as hunting and fishing occur in the autumn and spring. Guess where the students are? Interestingly, Sowell (1983) has made observations that reinforce the point about how statistics can be misleading. He notes that more members of classically disadvantaged groups in the United States are continuing on to college. He is quick to point out, however, that African, Mexican, and Puerto Rican Americans attend less demanding schools, attend lower quality colleges, and pursue degrees in academically less challenging and less prestigious fields, such as education. By contrast, Jewish, Chinese, and Japanese Americans attend demanding schools, more prestigious colleges, and pursue degrees in mathematics and the sciences.

Try as I might, and despite my inclination to celebrate all that different cultural communities have to offer, I believe that the positive "spin" put on the academic status of society's most disadvantaged groups is misplaced. Conditions are worse than the statistics portray, and the statistics alone are reason enough to sound the alarm. But as long as it appears that women are approaching men, African Americans are gaining on Whites, and Aboriginal students are making some improvement, then mainstream policymakers and educators need not confront the pedagogical, social, and moral issues.

Two features of the statistical reality require elaboration. First, it is clear that an explanation for the academic underachievement lies not with personal but with group characteristics and more generally intergroup relations. Moreover, it is not one particular disadvantaged group that should be the focus of analysis but rather what is common to all disadvantaged. That is, our liberal democratic values are rooted in individualism, and it is a genuine value in the sense that it asks that we focus attention on the rights, plight, and needs of every single individual. This focus on the individual ensures that no one is left out or behind. There are, therefore, very good reasons for people to be reluctant to lump people together in groups. But when there are genuine group differences, it is constructive to shift attention to the group level. To search for explanations at the individual level will, by definition, fail to capture what must genuinely be a group and intergroup issue.

The statistics make clear that groups who vary in terms of geographic location throughout North America, who live in isolated communities and reserves or crowded cities, who have retained their heritage language or function only in English or French, and whose racial heritages are dramatically different all show the same academic profile. Thus, any explanatory theory must focus on what experiences are shared by this wide variety of groups.

It could be argued that, while a variety of groups are disadvantaged, the cause of the disadvantage is different for each group. However, if that were true then we would expect each group to have a different profile of disadvantage. But the profiles for the different groups are surprisingly similar. For example, it is clear that academic underachievement does not surface in isolation. The reality is that the communities we are concerned about, as the statistics reveal, share an alarming array of social problems ranging from family instability and violence to substance misuse and suicide. The similarity to the profile shared by such disparate groups suggests that theory must be sought at a level that emphasizes the factors they share in common.

THE CHALLENGE OF EXPLAINING GROUP-BASED UNDERACHIEVEMENT

Thus far, I have only presented detailed statistics for the groups that experience persistent academic underachievement. In order to set the stage for understanding this profound social problem in the chapters to come, we need to place the question of academic achievement in a broader context. To do this, I have prepared a detailed table that lists a wide variety of groups along with an indication of whether their academic performance tends to be average, above average, or below average (Table 2.3).

For each group, I have noted certain key characteristics such as whether the group is White or non-White, whether the heritage language of the group is English, or a language other than English, and whether the heritage culture is European or not. The table is designed to serve as a reference point for evaluating various theories that have attempted to explain the academic underachievement of the groups that are the focus of the present volume. For example, it is clear from Table 2.3 that any simple racial explanation is inconsistent with reality. Many non-White groups perform as well or better than White mainstream North Americans. Similarly, it is clear that having a home language that is other than English poses no obvious difficulties. Finally, some groups whose heritage culture is other than European perform well academically.

Table 2.3
Summary of Academic Performance of Different Cultural Groups

Cultural Group	Color	Home Language	Heritage Culture	Academic Performance
WAS(P)	W	E	Euro	A
Jewish	W	E/NE	NonEuro/Euro	AA
Chinese	NW	E/NE	NonEuro	AA
Japanese	NW	E/NE	NonEuro	AA
Korean	NW	NE	NonEuro	AA
Filipino	NW	NE	NonEuro	AA
Sikh	NW	NE	NonEuro	AA
African American	NW	E	Euro	BA
Mexican American	NW	NE/E	NonEuro	BA
Puerto Rican	NW	NE	NonEuro	BA
Aboriginal (Inuit)	NW	NE/E	NonEuro	BA
Aboriginal	NW	NE/E	NonEuro	BA

Notes: W=White, NW=Non-White, E=English, NE=Non-English, Euro=European, NonEuro=Non-European, A=Average AA=Above Average, BA=Below Average.

Table 2.3 is, of necessity, only suggestive, because a number of complications arise when groups are categorized in any simple manner. In reality, there are problems with each of the categories described in Table 2.3. To begin with, even the group labels are problematic. For example, how do we refer to those who are part of mainstream, white, and presumably advantaged society? Does it include only those who descend from the British Isles, or does it include those from other western European nations who no longer identify themselves by their heritage nation? I have chosen the colloquial designation WASP to refer to White Anglo Saxon Protestant. I have bracketed the (P) to indicate that, certainly since John Kennedy was elected president, members of the Catholic faith would qualify equally.

Categorizing groups into White and non-White is problematic for two reasons. First, the non-White category includes any number of color variations ranging from brown to red to yellow to black, with every combination in between. Indeed, describing any group in purely racial terms is fallacious. Second, many groups involve members, some of whom categorize themselves as White, and others as non-White.

Caution needs to be exercised for the categorization of groups into differential academic performance. Direct comparisons are often unwarranted. The instruments used to gauge academic performance are not standard across studies, and potential confounding variables are often not considered. The social-class background of a student is one among a host of variables that would be crucial to control for in any direct comparison. Finally, academic performance for any group will not be homogenous, so that there will be great individual variation. The result is that, when referring to the performance of any particular group, the focus is on "average" performance. Clearly, any particular member of a group that performs poorly "on average" may well be not only close to but above the average for a group that is deemed to have good performance.

The "Home Language" category is also ambiguous. Naturally, we would expect people in Japan to have Japanese as their heritage language and those who are Navajo to have been raised in Navajo. But what of third- and fourth-generation Japanese Americans and Canadians? Is Japanese still their heritage language, or were they brought up in English? Our Navajo students may live in a community where the heritage language has been lost. The problem is that many studies do not specify clearly the home language of the students in question. Where in the table an English and non-English entry appears, it indicates that the academic performance of the group in general is not affected by the home language, be it English or the heritage language.

In addition, the home language category is an oversimplification. The dichotomous division into English and non-English does not capture the fact for some groups non-English refers to a world language such as, for example, Japanese. For other groups, non-English refers to a minority language as might be the case for Inuit, who speak Inuttitut, or Aboriginal Indian groups, who speak the language of their tribe, be it Cree, Mohawk, or any one of literally hundreds of Aboriginal languages.

Finally, my designation of the cultural heritage of groups into European and non-European is obviously done to counteract theories that emphasize the importance of European culture for success in formal schooling in North America. The problem is that it is never clear whether Eastern and Southern European heritage should be included in the European category or treated as separate categories.

With all of these disclaimers, why would I bother to present such an odious table that highlights differences between cultural groups? My reason is simple. The table, flawed as it is, leads to one inescapable conclusion. There is no simple and compelling racial, language, or cultural theory that neatly explains group differences in academic achievement. Any reader who believes that these factors singly or in combination are the cause of disadvantage are forced by the table to read on.

Street Kids

You can find them roaming the downtown streets of any major metropolis. They are called "street kids" or, more formally, homeless youths or street youths, and they look as bad as they probably feel. One of the surprising features of these young people is their relative gentleness. For the most part, they are nonviolent, submissive, and readily approachable.

The formal definition of a "street kid" is a young person who has no fixed, regular, and adequate nighttime residence. What this underscores is the difficulty associated with documenting the precise number of street kids in order to gain some appreciation for the magnitude of the problem. In Canada, estimates vary from 45,000 to 150,000 on any given day, and the figures in the United States can range up to 1.5 million. But these are guestimates at best. After all, most studies make their estimates by monitoring shelters, drop-in centers, and telephone crisis hotlines. Many street kids studiously avoid any contact with formal institutions, thus, making any census problematic. The more serious problem, of course, is that when studies of the attitudes, perceptions, motivations, and circumstances of street kids are conducted, they are recruited at shelters and drop-in centers. Are young people recruited in this manner truly representative of street kids?

Professionals make a number of distinctions in order to better understand the plight of these young people. While the basic distinction is often
made between throwaways and runaways, a more useful categorization
focuses on the conditions that led a young person to take to the streets.
From this perspective, family dysfunction is by far the most often cited reason for leaving home. A second category is more economic and arises when
the family is destitute and young people become separated from their parents because of divisions in social services. A final category involves resi-
dential instability, which arises following foster care when a young person
has no home to return to.

Not surprisingly, there are a host of characteristics that are predictably
associated with street life. Street kids lack nutritious food and suffer sleep
deprivation. Tattoos and body piercing are normative. Many have been
sexually abused, they tend to be sexually promiscuous, and suffer an inordinate number of sexually transmitted diseases. As well, substance misuse
is rampant, and many earn money through prostitution, panhandling,
squeegying car windows, selling drugs or minor theft.

Street kids are a particularly mysterious group in terms of their composition. You would expect that the ethnic composition of street kids would at
least mirror the ethnic composition of large metropolitan centers. If anything, given that poverty is more prevalent among certain visible minority
groups and that they tend to concentrate in the inner city, you would expect
to find few mainstream White young people living on the downtown
streets. Surprisingly, however, while street kids are by no means ethnically
homogeneous, the majority are White.

Mainstream North Americans have two very different, indeed competing, folk theories about street kids, a group of young people with whom
they have very little direct experience. The first "folk" theory is that these
are young people who have dropped out of mainstream society for a variety of sympathetic reasons, including a dysfunctional family environment,
mental illness, or systematic academic failure. Accordingly, these young
people need a supportive environment that, first, meets their basic needs
for food, shelter, and drug misuse. Equally important is their need for a
form of support that offers them the opportunity to gain a foothold in mainstream society. The assumption is that these young people are in a poor
state of physical and mental health. They, therefore, need more support
than other young people to get ahead, but once achieved, their physical and
psychological well-being will improve dramatically.

The second, and competing, folk theory that is popular among
mainstreamers is quite different. It assumes that these young people have
freely chosen to live on the streets, and have no interest in, or intention to,

engage in mainstream society. Street kids are viewed as embracing a life-style devoid of responsibilities and pressures: one that uses society's generosity as much as possible while obliviously but happily engaging in parties and drugs all the while. It is believed that they look to each other as a reference group, eschewing everything and anything that is valued by mainstream society.

These competing folk theories depict street kids in quite different ways. The first assumes they are motivated to join mainstream society and are in poor physical and mental health as they live aimlessly on the streets. The second believes them to be united in their rejection of mainstream society and, while they may be malnourished and addicted to drugs, they nevertheless are happy-go-lucky in a lifestyle they have freely embraced, if not chosen, for themselves.

Why Are "Street Kids" Included in This Book?

Other than being extremely disadvantaged, it would seem that on the surface street kids have nothing in common with the ethnic groups that I have singled out in this book. Their inclusion arises because of my conviction, based on my own research and experience, that neither of the two folk theories I have described explains the plight of these young people.

In terms of the first folk theory, street kids show no apparent interest in taking advantage of opportunities to reintegrate into mainstream society. Educational and job opportunities are not seized and the possibility for more stable housing is not pursued, even when the way is partially paved.

The folk theory that views street kids as a peer-oriented subculture, in opposition to mainstream society, does not fit either. Street kids do not form tight-knit groups that, no matter how non-normative from a mainstream perspective, seem to satisfy the human need for lasting relationships. In this sense, street kids are not like the urban gangs we hear about so much. Gangs, often described as providing their members with all the needs of a family, demand fierce and long-lasting loyalty. Such is not the case with street kids. Their friendships and intimate relationships are transitory and characterized by a great deal of mistrust. Most revealing is their relationship with pets. Many street kids have pet dogs that are adorned with a kerchief around their neck. Indeed, the drop-in center that I frequent has metal rings bolted to the floor of the large entranceway so that dogs can be tied up. I have often witnessed a young person, when presented with some food, sharing it with his or her dog. On more than one occasion, I have seen young people spend freshly panhandled money on medication for their dog when they seemed more in need of it than their pet. A popular analysis is that street kids are attracted to pets because pets offer unconditional love, something these young people so desperately need. Similarly, pets are totally dependent on their master, and thus the young person has at least some modest measure of control in a world largely out of control. And yet I have often seen pet dogs, the same ones who were lavished with "people" food, cast away for no apparent reason and with no visible remorse or regret.

That is why street kids are included here. They are an ethnic anomaly, and yet I believe they confront a psychological challenge that is similar to other severely disadvantaged groups.

Of Mainstream Women and Men

Young, middle-class White men and women virtually define advantage in a youth-oriented, racially biased society. I will propose a theory of "self" that emphasizes the collective identity component of self, a theory that is presumed to have universal applicability. Society's most disadvantaged groups confront, I believe, a crisis of collective identity. Mainstreamers, by virtue of their advantage, presumably do not. Indeed, when we document the crisis faced by the disadvantaged, it will seem that any challenges to the "self" experienced by mainstreamers pale by comparison.

I will argue that mainstreamers are forced to accommodate threats to their collective identity and, as mild as they may be by comparison, raising them serves two important functions. First, raising the potential for a malaise of self will hopefully make the theory and its implications more comprehensible. Second, and of greater importance, it may help mainstream readers to more fully appreciate the reality of the challenge faced by groups that are extremely disadvantaged.

In Chapter 1, I suggested that young mainstream men appear to be at a growing risk for the array of social ills that confront society's most severely disadvantaged groups. I purposely did not include statistics related to gender in the tables presented earlier because the situation for young mainstream men is quite different from the groups I have already discussed. Ironically, mainstream men are usually evoked as the advantaged peoples whose academic and social conditions are the standard against which severely disadvantaged groups are compared. Indeed, as the earlier tables illustrate, it is comparisons with society's advantaged groups that serve to define the magnitude of disadvantage.

The irony is compounded when we consider that mainstream men are also the advantaged standard that has and does serve to legitimize the discriminatory treatment of women. So how can I have the gall to suggest that young, mainstream, largely White men are disadvantaged?

My concern with young mainstream men arises from the following observations. Mainstream White men have been the most privileged group in

society, enjoying a very favorable status compared with disadvantaged minority groups and women. The women's movement has been, and contin-
ues to be, an uphill battle because women have been required to redefine
their role not merely because of but in spite of a powerful opponent, men.
But women have made gains, not to the point that total equality has been
achieved, but sufficient enough to disrupt the once comfortable and privileged role of men.

I will argue that the fallout from these ongoing changes has been on the
heads of young mainstream men, and to set the stage for my analysis, I have
presented some recent statistics, which are summarized in Table 2.4. What
the statistics point to is the hint of malaise that I believe is destined to grow.
Men experience more academic failure, they drop out of school at twice the
rate of women, they are more underemployed, and they have a higher rate
of successful suicide.

Table 2.4
Gender Differences in the United States and Canada

	Male	Female
Education		
Hight school dropouts (U.S.)	25.3%	18.2%
High school dropouts (Canada)	22%	14%
College enrollment of high school graduates (U.S.)		
1960	54.0%	37.9%
1998	62.4%	69.1%
College enrollment of high school graduates (Canada)	46%	54%
Employment		
Civilian labor force (U.S., per 1000)		
1960	46,388	23,240
1998	73,959	63,714
Civilian labor force (Canada, percent)		
1975	74%	41%
1993	65%	51%
Social Problems		
Suicide (U.S., per 100,000)	15.4	3.4
Delinquency rates (U.S., per 1000)	92.9	28.8

Sources: U.S. Census Bureau (2000); Statistics Canada (1993, 1994).

Conclusions

Academic underachievement and various forms of social dysfunction are problems that we attribute to the individual. That is not to say that we necessarily blame the individual for his or her problems. Some would hold the individual solely responsible, but others might point to the family, important institutions such as the school, the community, or society as a whole. But regardless of the explanation, the problem is analyzed by examining the factors that might explain the *individual's* predicament.

What I am emphasizing in this chapter is that, while problems are manifested by an individual, there is an inescapable association between a particular consortium of problems and group membership. The inescapable conclusion is that we must seek an explanation, not at the individual level but at the group and, by extension, the intergroup level.

CHAPTER 3

Collective Identity: A Person's Primary Psychological Blueprint

In this chapter, I lay the theoretical foundation for understanding the plight of society's most disadvantaged groups. The focus of my theoretical analysis is the unique human capacity we have for self-reflection, and I will offer a theory of self that I believe to be universal. Thus, in this chapter, emphasis will be placed on a universal application of the essential functions of self. In so doing, this chapter might appear to be taking a detour from the main challenge of understanding society's most disadvantaged groups. I can assure you that, once the basic theoretical building blocks are in place in the chapters to follow, attention can focus directly on the implications of my theory of self for society's most disadvantaged, and not so disadvantaged, groups.

The importance of the psychology of self, and the lack of consensus about its functioning, is reflected in the number of descriptive labels that have come into fashion. These include self-concept, self-image, self-schema, self-identity, social-identity, social-self, self-digest, selfhood, and the ever popular self-esteem. My first task, then, will be to reduce the confusion somewhat by defining the labels that I will be using for my analysis. I will then theorize about the functions of self, and here I will argue that, to date, too much attention has been focused on one of the more popular labels—self-esteem. Having provided a functional analysis of the self, I will then describe what would constitute a psychologically healthy self and what social conditions might serve to promote a functioning healthy self.

FOUR COMPONENTS OF THE SELF

The concept that forms the basis of my analysis is the "self-concept." This term is chosen to reflect the nature of the psychological construct that I believe is central to human functioning. People have the unique capacity to not only act and think but to reflect back on themselves and ask questions such as "Who am I"? Equally important is that people have an enduring sense of who they are. That is, I may behave very differently at a formal dinner than I do when telling a bedtime story to my young child. I may feel very differently when I score the winning touchdown (in my dreams) or break up with my lover. But despite these dramatically different behaviors and feelings, I still feel like "me."

The glue that holds "me" together through all my different thoughts, feelings, and actions is a psychological or mental picture of "me" that is integrated and clear even if I would have difficulty describing this mental picture of "me" that I have. It is this mental picture of "me" that I will refer to as the "self-concept."

I am not suggesting that what I have labeled the "self-concept" is all there is to the self; far from it. There are a myriad complex processes associated with self-knowledge and how that knowledge relates to memory and finally the processes by which the self-concept becomes translated into self-presentation, into the formation of attitudes, and ultimately into concrete behavior. My focus here is on the relatively stable mental template that each of us has that forms the backdrop or self-context for having effective commerce with our social environment.

The importance of our self-concept cannot be overestimated. Social psychologists have recognized from the very beginning that human behavior is not random but organized and purposeful. That is why psychologists have proposed, in addition to the self-concept, dozens of mental concepts to explain behavior: Attitudes, expectations, stereotypes, attributions, and traits are merely a small sampling. So why are mental concepts in general, and in our case the self-concept specifically, deemed to be so important? Without mental concepts, meaningful human behavior would be impossible. Take the simple experience of being a passenger in my friend's new car. When it comes to opening the door to get out, I have a mental blueprint about how to open the door, based on my accumulated experience with numerous car doors. My mental concept about car doors is the blueprint that guides my actions when I want to get out. Armed with this mental guide, I coolly reach for the handle, observe its orientation, and then successfully pull or push the latch. My mental concept was invaluable. Indeed the only time my "door concept" might fail me is if my friend's new car has a whole new mechanism. In that case, I will have to swallow my pride and ask the stupid question, "How do I get out of this thing?" If you want to observe simple mental concepts in operation, watch the ease with which a gasoline attendant approaches most cars to insert the nozzle, and then watch the same attendant when the gas port is in an unusual place.

My reason for describing this trivial example is to show that, even here, my mental concepts are essential guides to my behavior. Imagine how important my mental concepts are when it comes to behavior in the domain of performing my job, raising my children, and interacting with my partner. Given that my mental concepts are essential, can there be any more important concept than self-concept?

Self-concept, like all mental concepts, no doubt serves a number of important functions, but two are central to the present analysis. The two components or dimensions of self-concept I want to distinguish between are "identity" and "esteem." Identity is the component that describes who I am. By contrast, esteem is the component that forms my evaluation of myself. So, the overused phrase "low self-esteem" refers to a person who values his or her self-concept negatively. Thus, identity answers the question, "*Who* am I?" whereas esteem answers the question, "Am I *worthy?*"

What I am suggesting is that all our mental concepts serve two important functions, one cognitive and one emotional. The self-concept is no different. It is just more important because it is the construct that represents "me." The cognitive dimension is reflected by the identity dimension of the self-concept. In this sense, it serves as our own personal blueprint for action; it guides our thoughts, feelings, and actions in a coherent manner. The emotional or esteem dimension is reflected in the evaluative overtones associated with the self-concept. Self-esteem naturally arises from our constant evaluation of ourselves. Each little self-evaluation we make accumulates and ultimately becomes integrated to form a more global self-evaluation that emerges to form our self-esteem.

Before elaborating more on the identity and esteem components of the self-concept, a second distinction needs to be made. The distinction is one that has been elaborated on most coherently in a theory of social identity proposed by Tajfel and Turner (1979) and more recently in Turner's (1987) theory of self-categorization. The distinction involves a contrast between personal identity and social identity. Turner (1987) views the self-concept as involving elements that are "personal," in the sense that they refer to characteristics that are unique to the person. By contrast, social aspects of the self-concept involve those characteristics that a person shares with all other members of his or her group. This distinction is crucial to our analysis since we are particularly concerned with entire cultural groups who share a common set of problems.

My view of the self-concept can best be illustrated in the form of a two-dimensional diagram (see Figure 3.1).

From the diagram, we can see that by crossing the two dimensions of the self-concept (identity versus esteem by personal versus collective), we can distinguish four aspects of the self-concept. Each of these requires elaboration. The first quadrant points to the personal identity elements of the self-concept. Here I am referring to personal characteristics that do not evaluate but rather describe who I am. I am an intelligent, warm, athletic, and responsible person (again in my dreams). These are not merely characteristics but implied goals or end-states that define who I am. By identifying myself as intelligent, I see myself as someone whose goals in life, including the life's work I aspire to, will be an extension of the meaning associated with intelligence. The "intelligent" component of my personal identity does not specify precisely which goals I set for myself, nor does it guarantee me any success at achieving them. What it does do is provide me with a sense of general orientation and motivation to achieve them. Similarly, "warm" implies goals I have for my interpersonal relationships, and "athletic" orients me to physical activity. Again, it may not specify which sport I take up or if I will be any good at the sport, but it does orient and motivate me toward sporting activity.

Intelligence, warmth, and athleticism are characteristics, or a combination of characteristics, that set me apart as unique. Presumably, the only way for me to know that these are characteristics that are unique to me is by comparing myself to others and realizing that these are characteristics on which I tend to differ from the average or the majority. In order to make this comparison, I must have some reference group in mind. For example, if the personal identity aspect of my self-concept includes "intelligent," I am not

Figure 3.1
Four Aspects of the Self Concept

	SELF-CONCEPT	
	Identity	**Esteem**
Personal	Personal Identity	Personal (Self) Esteem
Collective	Collective Identity	Collective Esteem

comparing myself to Einstein or Hawking but rather to some impression of people who are similar to me, in short, my in-group. It is important to stress again that my personal identity is not limited to my unique personality characteristics: It includes by implication my own personal values, goals, my personal attitudes, and my own unique behavioral style.

When I engage the social comparison process, I do not have to be more intelligent or athletic than every single person in my group in order to include these characteristics in my identity. I just have to be more than average. Thus, there is room for more than one member of each group to be intelligent or athletic. Moreover, if I am below average on these abilities, I need not include "stupid" or "clumsy" in my identity. I may, but more likely these will be two domains I do not try building my identity around.

Once I have a clearly defined and stable personal identity, my universe becomes comprehensible and manageable. My personal identity orients me to the world around me. For example, it affects what I pay attention to because my personal identity tells me what I value. This is not a trivial issue. If I value a particular goal or end-state, then naturally I am motivated to achieve it. There are two components, in the sense that my personal identity defines my important goals and, thus, I am first energized and, second energized in a particular direction. If I had no clear characteristics and therefore no implied values or goals, I would have no direction, and hence I would be literally immobilized. The bottom line is that a clearly defined personal identity is necessary for effective and adaptive human functioning.

The second quadrant refers to my self-esteem in terms of the personal aspects of my self-concept. Here the focus is not on what my personal characteristics are but rather how I evaluate my characteristics. Again, in order to make an evaluation of myself, I will need to compare myself with others in terms of the characteristic in question. My own group, or relevant subgroups of my own group, is the most likely available reference point for such an evaluation.

It is important here to illustrate the genuine difference between personal identity and personal (self) esteem. My personal identity may include the characteristics "intelligent" and "athletic." You might conclude that my personal (self) esteem must automatically be extremely positive. First, there is the question of the extent to which I am successfully actualizing the characteristics in question. I might not be living up to my personal identity. Second, and more subtly, even if I am successfully actualizing my personal identity, a positive personal esteem is not guaranteed. For example, while it is generally true that in North American culture intelligence and athleticism are valued, such is not necessarily the case. Suppose the reference group I use to check on how my personal identity is evaluated downgrades people with these characteristics. Certain subgroups of high school students may judge me to be "nerdy," and "jocks" may have a negative reputation. The point is that knowing my personal identity does not automatically indicate my personal (self) esteem. I need to make a separate inquiry, or comparison, with my reference group to obtain evaluative feedback.

Quadrant three focuses on descriptive or identity aspects of my collective self-concept. Included here are characteristics I share with other members of my group. In the case of my ethnic group, this might include a shared history, shared values, shared goals, and a shared set of behaviors including, for example, the language we speak. Personality characteristics may also be involved to the extent that they are ones deemed to be applicable to most, if not all, members of my group. My ethnic group may perceive itself to be hardworking or intelligent. In this case, these personality characteristics would be included as part of my collective identity because these are characteristics that apply to all members of my group.

Without wishing to confuse the issue, it might be important to relate collective identity to ethnic stereotypes. I digress into stereotyping because it has been an enduring and central process for understanding ethnic relations. A stereotype involves consensus among members of one group about the characteristics of another: Italians are emotional, Germans are hardworking, the Scots are thrifty, Americans are imperialistic, and Canadians are boring. In our analysis of collective identity, we are not discussing how one group perceives another but rather how members of a group perceive themselves. Thus, we are referring to a special case of stereotyping where members of a group attribute characteristics to their own group, a phenomenon that has its own label, the autostereotype. Historically, scientists and policymakers alike viewed stereotyping as a destructive social process. Stereotyping was judged destructive on two grounds. First, stereotyping was judged to be an inferior cognitive process because it involves applying a group-based perception indiscriminately to each and every member of another group. Second, stereotyping was felt to be morally wrong because it categorized individuals who have no desire to be categorized.

Current theorizing about stereotypes is far less ideologically laden. For example, while no one is suggesting that stereotyping a group with blatantly negative characteristics is desirable, there is some appreciation for the fact that people act as "cognitive misers," taking intellectual shortcuts when processing stimuli in their environment. Thus, we all stereotype people just as we might categorize any aspect of our environment in order to render the stimulus complexity and overload manageable. Similarly, it is clear that there are circumstances when I want to be categorized into a group. I may complain about my university not providing me with a big enough and aesthetically pleasing environment, but at academic conferences I am proud to be categorized and stereotyped as someone from McGill University.

Surely, if an ethnic group were stereotyped in a manner that it wished to be characterized, then we would view the process of stereotyping quite differently. Indeed, when governments and educators promote multiculturalism, so that ethnic groups are encouraged to retain their heritage culture, are they not promoting stereotypes? That is, are they not encouraging groups to display their culture, or ethnic identity, proudly (autostereotype) and in so doing ask that other groups stereotype them in a manner consistent with their chosen ethnic identity or autostereotype?

When stereotyping is viewed in this manner, it loses its negative overtones. When the autostereotype genuinely reflects a group's ethnic identity, then it may be serving to clarify a group's collective identity.

Finally, quadrant four refers to self-esteem that arises from group membership, collective self-esteem. In the case of personal self-esteem, the individual compares himslef or herself to other ingroup members. In the case of collective self-esteem, the individual compares his or her group with other groups. The result of the comparison indirectly determines its evaluative impact on the individual. I say indirectly because when I compare my own group to another group, the resulting comparison does not refer to me personally but to my group as a whole. However, I am a member of my group; I am by extension and inclusion impacted by the intergroup comparison. When a sports team wins the championship, it has a positive effect on the players, their fans, and indeed the entire city. Did not Donovan Bailey, by winning a gold medal for Canada in the 100-meter event, have this effect in the 1996 Olympic games? He performed as an individual against other individuals. He proved to be the fastest "individual" in the world. But we made it an intergroup comparison—one nation against other nations—and we won. Returning to our focus, members of a disadvantaged minority group may accumulate feedback that leads to low collective self-esteem every time they make comparisons of their group with advantaged outgroups.

The self-concept, then, comprises four components that become integrated to form the individual's complete mental image of himself or herself. The integration of the four components can provide insight into the psychological complexity the individual might have to cope with. For example, someone might have high personal self-esteem, but his or her membership in a disadvantaged minority group might mean that this individual also has a low collective self-esteem. More destructively, a person may have an unclear collective identity and we might wonder whether for such a person it would even be possible to have an identity that is clear at the personal level.

The Primacy of Collective Identity

My analysis of the self-concept thus far has not produced any novel propositions. The four components I have described are derived from distinguishing between identity and esteem, on one hand, and personal and collective identity on the other. These are distinctions that have been made previously and more eloquently by a number of other "self" theorists.

What I am about to propose, however, is novel and forms the essence of my argument in terms of understanding society's most disadvantaged. I propose that a person's collective identity is the most important and psychologically primary component to the self-concept. Personal identity involves individuals comparing themselves with members of their own group in order to determine what characteristics make them unique. Similarly, personal self-esteem requires that the individual make evaluative comparisons with his or her own group. How can an individual possibly develop personal identity and personal self-esteem in the absence of a clearly defined collective identity? Without a collective identity, the individual has no clearly established template upon which to articulate a personal identity or personal self-esteem. Thus, while all four components of the self-concept are crucial, collective identity takes psychological precedence.

What I am proposing runs counter to most current thinking about the "self." The usual analysis focuses attention on the individual and her or his personal identity and esteem. I am arguing explicitly that this emphasis is counterproductive. Logically, it is impossible to form a personal identity without a collective identity to serve as a reference point. This makes collective identity the key component to the self-concept. And this primacy has profound implications. Free will, the belief that individuals make choices and are responsible for those choices, is as central a belief as there is. Presumably, an individual's choices in life are extensions of his or her personal identity. But personal identity can only be articulated against the backdrop of a clearly defined collective identity.

If collective identity is psychologically primary to personal identity, so too is personal identity a necessary precursor to personal esteem. It is impossible to develop personal esteem without a personal identity because without identity there would be no concrete characteristics upon which to obtain evaluative feedback.

Thus, collective identity is rationally and psychologically primary, and therefore is the most important component of the self-concept. For groups that have a well-defined collective identity, attention naturally turns to personal identity and esteem. But when collective identity is compromised in any way, the entire self-concept is jeopardized.

The primacy of collective identity and its relationship to the other three components of the self-concept is captured schematically in the following diagram (see Figure 3.2).

COLLECTIVE IDENTITY IN THE CONTEXT OF CURRENT THEORIES OF THE SELF

The emphasis I have placed on collective identity becomes clear when making a contrast with other influential theories of the self. What I wish to underscore is that even those theories of self that do emphasize constructs that resemble my definition of collective identity make a fundamental assumption that needs to be challenged.

Figure 3.2
Relationship Between Collective Identity and the Self-Concept

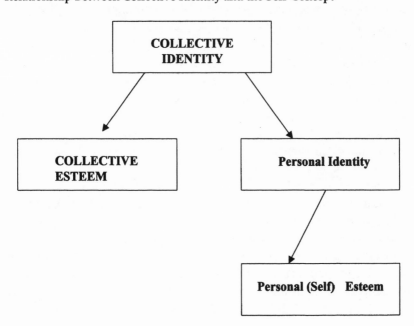

We begin with what Wicklund and Gollwitzer (1982) termed their theory of "symbolic self-completion." Their thesis is that, when an individual is committed to a particular self-definition, he or she is motivated to achieve completeness. Completeness involves making sure that the self-definition in question becomes an enduring and predictable aspect of the self. Individuals who are "incomplete," according to the theory, feel a psychological tension that motivates them to find a route, symbolic or real, that will allow for completeness.

But notice that the theory takes as its point of departure an apparently clearly articulated self-definition that is in need of completion. My question is, what about those who do not have a self-definition to begin with?

A clearer example is provided by Higgins (1987) who has proposed that there are three important "selves" that serve as essential guides in a person's life. He begins with the usual "actual" self, which is the person's own perception of who they are. He then adds the "ideal" self, which is the person's perception of the way he or she would ideally like to be, and the "ought" self, which is the person's view of the way he or she should be.

Higgins's (1987) self-discrepancy theory makes specific predictions about the consequences that arise when persons find a discrepancy between their "actual" self and their "ideal" self, and between their "actual" self and their "ought" self. Specifically, he proposes that falling short of one's "ideal" self will evoke unpleasant, low-arousal emotions, such as sadness and depression, whereas not matching one's "ought" self will give rise to unpleasant, high-arousal emotions, such as anxiety and anger.

My own analysis of self-discrepancy theory involves taking issue with certain assumptions that Higgins makes. He takes for granted the psychological reality of an "ideal" and "ought" self. Where do these components of the self come from? They must be socially defined. That is, how one "ought" to be involves internalizing the community's template for appropriate behavior, and for a self to be defined as "ideal," it must be a goal that society values. A clearly defined collective identity, then, provides the shared values that allow a person the opportunity to internalize an "ideal" and "ought" self.

When Higgins conducts experiments to test his theory, he uses university students who no doubt have a clearly defined collective identity. As such, they can articulate the different components of their "self," and discrepancies among the three components can be readily studied. But what of groups that have no clearly defined collective identity? How can they develop "ideal" and "ought" selves and then engage in the process of self-comparison and experience the motivational consequences of such a process? My argument is that they cannot, and that is why I propose that a clearly defined collective identity is a necessary prerequisite to the normal process involving the self that people engage in.

I would take similar issue with Swann's (1990) self-verification theory. He and others (for example, Sedikides & Strube, 1995) have been influential in demonstrating that people are not only motivated to maintain a favorable view of the "self" but are also interested in maintaining a consistent "self." Thus, for example, Swann has been able to show that people with a negative self-image actually seek negative information about themselves and reject positive feedback: People are not only motivated to achieve a favorable self, they are also interested in having their "self" verified.

Again, in order to engage in the process of self-verification, it is necessary to have a clearly defined self, otherwise there would be no basis for deciding which information did or did not verify the self. Thus, a clearly defined collective identity is a necessary prerequisite for processes involving self-verification.

My own view of the self in no way detracts from the contributions of theories focusing on self-discrepancy, self-verification, and self-affirmation theories. My concern is that they presuppose the existence of a clear definition of self. For severely disadvantaged groups, such an assumption may not be valid, which would leave members of such groups unable to engage these basic psychological processes associated with the self.

As a final example, I turn to Claude Steele's (1988) theory of self-affirmation. Steele conceives the self-concept as an image of self that strives to provide the individual with a sense of overall competence and morality. In this sense, Steele's conception is consistent with the underlying assumptions of all models of the self. Steele's unique contribution is his insight into how a person responds to specific threats to his or her self-image. Specifically, people worry less about combating the specific threat and focus instead on affirming the *central* component to their self-concept. As Steele remarks, "It is the war, not the battle, that orients this system" (Steele, 1988 p. 289).

This important adaptive process is, of course, predicated on the assumption that the individual has a clearly defined cluster of central elements that define the self. Presumably, without such a template, an individual is in no position to engage the all-important affirmation process. Quite simply, the individual has nothing to affirm.

Culture as a Special Case of Collective Identity

Culture is one of the most elusive yet obviously important and popular concepts in both everyday and scientific discourse. How many groups in the world today are struggling to protect their culture? Why is it that you apparently cannot destroy culture either at the point of a gun or with positive inducements to replace one's own culture with another that has more material resources to offer? Why is culture so important to protect yet difficult to define?

The answers to these questions arise out of my theory of the self-concept, and are important to the present analysis because most of the groups who are the focus of the present volume would be defined as ethnic or cultural groups.

Although definitions of culture vary widely, there is agreement about two features. First, culture is socially defined. That is, culture arises when members of a group come to share the same values, attitudes, beliefs, and behavioral patterns. Second, there is agreement that culture is not tangible and so is extremely difficult to define concretely.

Let us return to the component of the self-concept that I argued is the psychological bedrock: collective identity. I defined collective identity as that descriptive aspect of the self-concept that the individual shares with every member of one's group. This shared feature is precisely what makes collective identity a socially defined process and, in this sense, is identical to culture.

But what is so special about the domain of collective identity in the domain of culture, for, after all, collective identity refers to all my group identities, not just my cultural group. I may have a collective identity for any of the groups I belong to: my professional role group, my leisure group, or my geographic community. Collective identity need not be large and may involve an informal friendship group. Check out any high school and you will marvel at the distinct friendship cliques. They each have their own dress, ways of interacting, and special language. An outsider can not even follow their conversation, which is, after all, their aim: to form a special collective identity.

A collective identity can even emerge from as few as two people. Think of two people who fall madly in love and enter a long-lasting relationship. They quickly develop their own unique "love-expression" and special ways of communicating with each other. Before long, they have articulated their own special collective identity.

But culture is a very special form of collective identity. For example, my professional role identity may provide me with a blueprint in terms of job-related activities, but my cultural identity provides me with a blueprint for everything. It equips me with a template for family structure, child rearing, appropriate conduct with members of the opposite sex and elders, social rules governing how to cope with death, occupational structure and status, and explanations for the unknown, just to name a few. Thus, culture is socially defined and represents the individual's most pervasive and all-inclusive collective identity.

Some would argue that religious identity or national identity is as pervasive and all-inclusive as cultural identity. I would agree, but only under specific circumstances. Most religions do offer a blueprint for every dimension of life. If a religion is primary in a person's life, and especially where that religion applies to a circumscribed cultural group, then the two are interchangeable. Often, a religion will apply equally to a wide variety of cultural groups, in which case either may become primary or, more often, the religious identity will be incorporated into cultural identity. *Primary* for the present purposes, refers to the breadth of life dimensions over which it has influence.

The case of national identity is even more clear-cut. If nationality and ethnic group coincide, then the two identities may be interchangeable. But most nations are multicultural, and while national identity may touch many aspects of a person's life, it is cultural identity that is the more pervasive.

Thus, cultural identity deserves special status because it is usually the most pervasive collective identity and, therefore, the one that forms the basis for, and subsumes all other collective identities and, by extension, a person's personal identity.

Second, collective identity, like culture, is intangible precisely because it is a psychological concept that resides in the minds of individual group members. When members of a group share the same geographic space, have their own institutions, and share a history, they have the key ingredients for a clearly defined collective identity. Where group members are dispersed geographically or do not have the benefit of their own institutions, naturally they have to make an extra effort to maintain a clear collective identity.

Ironically, groups with the most favorable social conditions for collective identity, and whose collective identity is not threatened or challenged by outside groups or circumstances, are the ones that have the most difficulty describing their cultural identity. It is such a natural and ingrained collective identity that no one needs to think about their cultural identity or list its key ingredients.

Thus far I have referred to culture in terms of its structure and function with little comment on specific elements that are often associated with culture. Let us begin with one of the more controversial elements, language. Every time I ask members of an Aboriginal group to define their culture, the importance of their heritage language surfaces. Those who speak the heritage language claim it is the most important element of culture, whereas those who do not, opine, with some guilt, that it is important but not essential.

Language always surfaces in an exercise I conduct with Aboriginal teachers in communities where the heritage language is spoken by virtually everyone. I pose a series of questions that take the form, "If you did not ———, would you still be Inuit?" The blank gets filled in with everything from hunting and cooking to altering hairstyle to ceremonies to language. In every case, the answer is, "Of course I would still be Inuit," until it comes to the question of their heritage language, Innuttitut. This is the only point at which there is hesitation, with the majority concluding that, without their language, they might lose their identity and no longer be Inuit. The hesitation arises because they recognize that in many Arctic communities, the heritage language has been lost. Nevertheless, no one doubts that they are Inuit.

My own view is that language is *not* essential for culture, but it is extremely important. I would argue that there is no single element that is required for culture. A group's collective identity or culture is socially defined by the group, and, thus, it is for the group to decide which elements are essential, which are optional, and which are irrelevant.

Why, then, is language so often accorded such special cultural status? There are, I believe, very good reasons for language's preeminence. I have already noted how culture is an invisible mental construct. Language is one of the few tangible manifestations of collective identity. There are, of course, other visible manifestations of culture, such as ceremonies and dress, but language is one that is socialized from birth and, unlike other visible signs of culture, language requires a great deal of effort to master. Moreover, it is extremely difficult to attain nativelike fluency without any trace of accent. Language has another very important feature. As the mechanism for communication, it is an aspect of culture that is exclusive to members of the culture and one that permits private communication among members of a cultural group. For these reasons, language, while not absolutely essential to culture, is nevertheless extremely important.

I would go further and argue that the more a collective identity is threatened, the more important the role of language is for cultural identity. Minority groups, whose collective identity risks being swamped by more powerful cultures, are especially vigilant in protecting their heritage language. It is the one visible and exclusive element of culture that, as the vehicle for communication, binds the group together. Those few Aboriginal groups that have retained their heritage language guard it jealously, and those whose language is endangered are attempting restoration. In Canada, for example, it is estimated that of 53 Aboriginal groups, only the Cree, Ogibway, and the Inuit have any chance of having their language survive.

The Canadian province of Quebec protects the French language with pervasive laws that promote French as the language of the province. Newcomers to Quebec must send their children to French schools, companies must operate in French, professionals must pass a French exam, and public signs must be predominantly in French.

By contrast, people in North America, for whom English is their heritage language, are not particularly vigilant in promoting their language as part of their culture. Why not? Quite simply, Aboriginal people and French-speaking Quebecers are minority groups who must protect their culture to ensure its survival, whereas most English-speaking groups are in the majority with little fear of suffering cultural imperialism.

Interestingly, where English-speaking groups are culturally threatened, as is the case for those in Miami, Florida, where the Spanish language and culture are represented in high numbers and in French-dominated Quebec, Canada, the issue of English language and culture is a salient one. The English-speaking minority in the province of Quebec openly expresses the threat it feels. For more than 20 years, the English minority has unceasingly railed against what it believes to be repressive laws designed to promote French and in their minds, to sabotage the English language and, by extension, the English-speaking community.

Witness the growing "English Only" movement in the United States. Until recently, English was unquestionably the language of America. Minority language groups were encouraged to use their language in order to feel more comfortable in America and minority languages were an integral part of bilingual education programs because these programs helped minority youngsters to ultimately perform better in English at school. The backlash surfaced when the number of Spanish-speaking minority groups reached a critical mass, with the projection that by the middle of this century, the Hispanic community will triple and language minority groups will actually outnumber the White population.

The result is that presently, 23 states have declared English as the official language. In California, where there is a sizeable Hispanic community, bilingual Spanish-English programs have been summarily shut down. The result is a return to requiring Spanish-speaking students to be submerged in English schooling. Ironically, this is precisely the process that proved so detrimental to Hispanic students that it gave rise to bilingual education programs in the first place.

In summary, I would argue that language is a central component of identity for members of groups whose collective identity is under threat but less important for those whose collective identity is secure. Thus, the centrality of language for identity is a function of the identity status of a group; as the clarity and security of group's collective identity changes so too will the role that language plays for identity.

In contrast to the importance of language for culture, I want to comment briefly on those apparently superficial aspects of culture that are not often considered in the context of culture. I am referring to those little cultural habits ranging from the details of a church service or the flags that adorn buildings to the rituals involved with meals or the way we greet each other. None of these elements constitutes the core values or beliefs associated with a culture; they are tiny ways of doing things that become so ingrained that we never think of them and certainly never consider them essential. But their importance is revealed once they are disrupted. When you exchange "good mornings" with a colleague every day for 30 years, it becomes a ritual that goes completely unnoticed until one day when your colleague does not reciprocate the "good morning" ritual. You will spend the rest of the day preoccupied with why your colleague failed to reciprocate the "good morning" ritual. National flags that adorn so many buildings fly unnoticed until some group takes it upon itself to burn the nation's flag. I can still remember when the Catholic Church permitted services to be conducted in English instead of Latin. People were shocked when elderly parishioners opposed the change and wanted a return to Latin, even though they understood no Latin. And when, at the weekly Sunday family dinner, mother changes the menu, you would think she had committed highway robbery.

What these anecdotes illustrate is that an important element of culture is the hundreds of familiar behaviors that are trivial in their own right but that accumulate to create a sense of social familiarity, comfort, and meaning that is essential. There is room in collective identity for little rituals.

In summary, our focus in this volume is on groups that are often described as cultural groups, and I have argued that we need to address their problems at the group level. Thus, culture must figure prominently in our analysis, and I would define culture as the collective identity component of the self-concept.

Self-Esteem: An Overused Construct

Virtually every difficulty that people face, be it academic under achievement, problems with interpersonal relationships, or social violence, is blamed on low self-esteem. Indeed, all we need to do is tune in to Oprah Winfrey or flip through the pages of *Cosmopolitan* to become convinced that promoting high self-esteem will cure every personal and interpersonal ill. And society has bought into the concept. The following quote from a California State task force underscores the importance that society confers on the notion of high self-esteem: "Self-esteem might function as a social vaccine to inoculate individuals against the lures of crime, violence, substance abuse, teen pregnancy, child abuse, chronic welfare dependency and educational failure. The lack of self-esteem is central to most personal and social ills plaguing our state and nation " (page 4, 1990).

Children in school are force-fed the notion that each and every one of them is a superstar, and in case there is any doubt, teachers stick stars on every piece of work they produce. I have witnessed it firsthand while coaching a young boy's ice hockey team. Coaches were encouraged to teach the boys not to compete with one another. Specifically, this meant not keeping score of which team scored the most goals and publicly proclaiming every player to be a superstar. How ludicrous. If the league was serious about eliminating competition, it would not dress teams in different colors, and it would have given each and everyone of the 12 players on the ice a hockey puck to doodle with. But as soon as you have two teams, two goals, and one puck, it is a competitive structure that no one, especially young boys who love the game of hockey, can ignore. And every player on my team was acutely aware of precisely how good, or limited, he was as a player in terms of hockey prowess without me ever saying a word. They scoffed openly at hockey tournaments when every player on every team won a medal. The artificial promotion of high self-esteem failed miserably.

To be fair, social psychologists are coming to recognize that high self-esteem may have been an over simplistic antidote to all of society's ills. Indeed, there is even some suggestion that certain forms of high self-esteem may be psychologically destructive. When an individual has an inflated self-esteem that is coupled with an esteem that is unstable or vulnerable, the psychological effects may be maladaptive with a particular penchant for violence. Coping with a less than extremely positive self-image may be a challenge, but it may be worse to entertain an extremely high opinion of yourself only to have the image shattered by any life event that challenges such a lofty view of the self.

Without wishing to discount the importance of self-esteem, I would like to redress the balance by developing a thorough appreciation for the second important dimension of the self-concept: identity.

Identity focuses on the question of who I am. Having a clear notion of what I value, the goals I strive for, what attitudes I espouse, the activities I enjoy, and my behavioral style is essential in guiding my life. My identity locates me in social space and orients me to the world I live in so that I can have effective commerce with my environment. Without a clear identity, I have no direction, no goal, no purpose, and no sense that I am an integrated person.

If we are ever to successfully foster a clear identity in people, it is essential that we appreciate how our definition of self develops. The simple but profound answer is that identity is socially defined. When I need to know whether to dress warmly, carry an umbrella (which I never do anyway), or jump off a cliff, I look to the physical environment for the appropriate information. But where do I look when I want to know what values to hold, what attitudes to adopt, or how to distinguish right from wrong, good from bad, or how to treat people and what to devote my life to? There is no physical reality to turn to for an answer. Values cannot be found in the wind, morals are not under the snow, and justice is not forged in granite. The only source of information upon which I can build my identity is other people. Other people, be they my parents, friends, political leaders, teachers, or my cultural group, are the only sources I can turn to. Sometimes I may not rely on people directly. My fundamental rights and my beliefs in democracy and justice may be written in legislation, constitutions, or commandments. But it was people that composed and defined what now appears in legislation. Indeed, legal scholars recognize that informal social norms precede so-called black ink law. Clearly, not every socially defined norm becomes enshrined in law but only those that are deemed to be important for group functioning and where there is a group consensus about the behavior in question.

If people are the source or raw material upon which we build our identity, the oft quoted line, "No man (woman?) is an island" takes on greater significance. First and foremost, each of us needs commerce with people in order to build an identity. This does not mean that we automatically enter every piece of information from others into our self-concept. Presumably, we compare, think about, select, and reject information. But ultimately, without others we cannot even engage in the process of building our definition of self.

My seemingly straightforward analysis forces us to confront many widely held beliefs. For example, teenagers are encouraged to, "Just say no" when pressured to try drugs. What our analysis makes clear is that such a demand on teenagers flies in the face of everything we know about building identity. As we have seen, others are a vital source of our most important information; commerce with them is essential and their views may be rejected, but they must be taken seriously. The point here is that asking teenagers to ignore the views of others is both unnatural and impossible.

This brings us to the broader issue of conformity in general. Society and social scientists alike, particularly in Western culture, take a dim view of those who conform to others. Those who are influenced by others are regarded as sheep who are somehow incapable of thinking for themselves. But as we have come to appreciate, we all rely on others for information that is critical to the development of our identity. Asking us not to conform is asking us to eschew our only source of information on what matters to us most. Without positioning myself to be influenced by others, I may know when to carry an umbrella, but I will never be able to establish my own set of values and rules for living that can guide me in every situation I might confront.

The real question is not should I conform, but rather whom should I conform to? We are all conformists. What differentiates us is whom we conform to when establishing our identity. Teenagers should not be counseled to just say no but rather to expand their array of potential sources of information. We began our analysis with the aim of gaining an appreciation for the importance of the identity dimension of the self-concept. My argument is simply that too much attention has been paid to the esteem dimension, with a corresponding neglect of identity. I would even go so far as to suggest that without a clear identity, or definition of self, it is not even possible to engage in the process of self-evaluation. How can I know if I am doing well if I do not know who I am or what kind of person I am aiming to be? How can I evaluate my intelligence if I have no idea whether or not intelligence has any relevance for me?

My aim is not to belittle the importance of self-esteem but to have us appreciate the role of identity. A clearly defined personal and collective identity provides the person with a blueprint and framework, which provides meaning to that person's every thought, feeling, and action.

I would propose that we stop evoking self-esteem as the panacea for every personal problem. Instead, we need to focus on the identity dimension of self-concept in order to make constructive interventions. When children are underachieving at school, maybe we need to spend more time helping them with formulating a clear identity and less time artificially bolstering their self-esteem. After all, self-esteem is meaningless in the face of no clearly defined identity.

Self-Regulation Failure

Recently, social psychologists have turned their attention to processes related to self-regulation. Baumeister and Heatherton (1996) begin their influential review of this literature with the observation that, "Modern American society suffers from a broad range of problems that have self-regulation failure as a common core. Crime, teen pregnancy, alcoholism, drug addiction, venereal disease, educational underachievement, gambling, and domestic violence are among the social problems that revolve around the apparent inability of many individuals to discipline and control themselves."

This constellation of social problems that the authors associate with modern America are rampant in the severely disadvantaged communities that we are concerned with here. I believe that my thesis about the primacy of collective identity has been underappreciated by those who focus on the psychology of self-regulation.

The very term *self-regulation* is predicated on the assumption that individuals confront difficult behavioral choices, otherwise there would be no need for each of us to regulate our behavior. The essence of a choice involving the need for "regulation" arises when the individual must choose between immediate gratification with long-term costs versus regulating, or not responding to immediate gratification with the firm belief that benefits will accrue in the long term. I won't eat that doughnut now so that in the future my weight will drop, I won't get drunk now so that I can ensure good long-term job performance, I won't react to an insult with physical violence in order to avoid long-term negative repercussions, and I will study for my test with a view to the long-term career payoffs.

Put differently, failures in self-regulation occur when an individual does not act in a manner that is consistent with his or her standards or ideals. Smoking, overeating, excessive gambling, substance abuse, and violence are all negatively valued behaviors that all require self-regulation, because in certain circumstances each is highly attractive—if they were not, there would be no need for self-regulation.

Baumeister and Heatherton do a thorough job of categorizing the processes that might lead an individual to fail in his or her attempts to self-regulate when confronted with an immediately gratifying circumstance. They discuss only briefly the role that culture might play in the process. Essentially, they acknowledge that to the extent that a culture loosens its normative demands in areas where self-regulation is needed, it makes it easier for individuals to not live up to their own internalized standards and ideals. My argument about the primacy of collective identity would build on this acknowledgement considerably. Failures in self-regulation, ranging from smoking and overeating to academic underachievement and violence, are genuine social issues that are central to collective identity. That is, there is widespread agreement about what behaviors need to be self-regulated, and surely most individuals internalize these as standards and ideals precisely because the collective (cultural) identity spells them out as undesirable behaviors.

Where a collective identity is unclear, individual group members are not under great pressure to adopt self-regulated standards and ideals. Naturally, failures of self-regulation will be widespread. Baumeister and Heatherton began their review by noting the widespread failures in self-regulation in certain domains. Their analysis, however, focuses on individual differences in self-regulation. Surely, when failures are widespread, the issue is a social one.

My argument would be that the source of the rampant failure in self-regulation found in disadvantaged communities is the lack of a clearly defined collective identity, a collective identity that spells out precisely what behaviors need regulation, thereby ensuring that individuals internalize them. Such internalization in no way guarantees that failures will not occur, but it surely makes it more difficult for each individual to not do his or her best at regulating non-normative behavior.

Conclusions

I have argued that the self-concept is the pivotal building block for understanding the problems confronted by society's most disadvantaged groups. Crucial to understanding the self is a distinction between the identity and esteem elements, and the personal and collective dimension of the self-concept. I propose that collective identity, of which cultural identity is the most all-inclusive, is the most important component of the self. As such, I believe that the concept self-esteem has been accorded more importance than it deserves.

The ideal self-concept for effective human functioning is one that begins with a clearly defined collective identity and from that base builds a clear personal identity along with a favorable personal and collective esteem. In the chapters that follow, I will describe the social processes that conspire to disrupt peoples' self-concept, especially their collective identity.

CHAPTER 4

Traditional Explanations for Group Differences: The Usual Suspects

Armed with our theory emphasizing collective identity, we are in a position to return more directly to the matter at hand. Important group-based differences are what we need to explain. A necessary starting point for our journey toward understanding is the evolution of theory designed to explain the academic underachievement and social dysfunction represented by our target groups. The journey is a rocky one, for it is as much an emotional as an intellectual voyage. That is, contained in any theory of group-based differences in achievement are fundamental assumptions that are laden with potential ideology, blatant prejudice, and implied self-serving social policy and political rhetoric. Imagine the possibilities when advantaged social scientists begin theorizing about why their group has been hugely successful in terms of power and technological advancement while other groups lag way behind.

Three discernible shifts in broad theoretical orientation can be delineated. The first theory to emerge argued simply that disadvantaged groups were genetically inferior to more advantaged groups. In North America and Europe, this meant that Whites were deemed to be genetically superior to people of color. Needless to say, such theorizing played into the hands of a White supremacy ideology with the result that the data produced to support a genetic argument were not scrutinized carefully.

The impetus for genetically based theories was the testing movement, which revealed that, with respect to intelligence (IQ) tests in particular, certain minority groups performed consistently less well than mainstream groups. A hot debate followed, since intelligence is believed to be the very essence of being human. From this debate arose cultural "deficit" theories; minority group cultures were inferior to mainstream culture, and these deficits prevented minority students from performing well on IQ tests and from succeeding in school. Finally, cultural deficit theories gave way to cultural "difference" theories, the proposition that no one group's culture is better or worse than any other. The underachievement of certain groups is mainly due to the cultures of these groups being different from mainstream culture. Because formal schooling was designed to be an extension of mainstream culture, other cultures are at a disadvantage.

It is tempting to trace "genetic" to "deficit" to "difference" theories as a linear progression of thought in the social sciences. While such a progression is parsimonious, it is unfortunately an oversimplification. Indeed, proponents of genetically based and cultural deficit theories continue to be influential and, hence, it will be important to briefly review the bases of each theoretical position. And the review is far more than an academic exercise because the implications for the very structure of formal education lie in the balance.

Genetic Theories

Genetically based theories of intelligence assume that certain minority groups do not possess the appropriate genes for high intellectual performance and, as a consequence, do poorly in school and are less suited to a progressive society. Just when such theories appear to be scientifically and politically obsolete, they resurface and generate an emotionally charged debate about the nature of human intelligence. Heated charges and countercharges followed the genetic arguments of group-based intelligence by Jensen in 1969 and Rushton in 1988, with the most recent resurgence being instigated by Herrnstein and Murray's (1994) controversial book, *The Bell Curve*. So provocative was their thesis that the Board of Scientific Affairs of the American Psychological Association felt compelled to commission an authoritative report on the issue.

The report was written by a blue ribbon panel composed of Neisser, Boodoo, Bouchard, Boykin, Brody, Ceci, Halpern, Loehlin, Perloff, Sternberg, and Urbina (1996) and attempted to, in an as objective fashion as possible, establish what is known and what is not known about the nature of human intelligence. On the surface, it is tempting to dismiss the entire controversy as purely academic, for, after all, who cares if individuals or entire groups perform differently on a "bunch of stupid tests." The problem is that these "bunch of tests" produce scores that are relatively stable during development and are predictive of school performance and years of education. Moreover, the tests correlate with occupational status, social status, and income. They even correlate with job performance and are implicated in socially undesirable social behaviors, such as juvenile crime. Thus, how individuals and groups score on standard intelligence tests must be taken seriously because, despite our limited understanding of the nature of these tests, they are related to a wide range of life domains that are highly valued in society.

What cannot be ignored is that some ethnic groups perform better on IQ tests than others. Specifically, while White Americans do relatively well, certain Hispanic groups (Mexican and Puerto Rican Americans) do less well on average and African Americans perform least well. There is insufficient research to be confident about the performance of Aboriginal people, but their performance appears to be consistently and dramatically lower than that of White North Americans.

The performance of different ethnic groups in terms of IQ tests does not always correspond to school achievement. For White, Mexican, Puerto Rican, and African Americans, performance on IQ tests is mirrored by their performance in school. Anomalies arise for Asian Americans and at least one study involving Aboriginal people. In the case of Asian American students, they perform at about the same level as Whites on standard IQ tests but in terms of achievement at school they excel. Conversely, Aboriginal groups such as the Inuit of Arctic Quebec have the lowest level of school performance of any sizable ethnic group. However, in a recent study by Wright, Taylor and Ruggiero (1996), a relatively large sample of Inuit students, living in a remote village and whose first language is Innuttitut, performed equal to or marginally better than age-appropriate United States and Canadian norms on a standardized test of intelligence.

Neisser and colleagues' (1996) analysis regarding these ethnic group differences in intelligence is less than conclusive. What is clear is that both heredity and the environment contribute to intelligence. Neisser and collegues (1996) conclude that there is little direct evidence for a genetic interpretation of ethnic group differences, but they admit that, to date, it is not clear what aspects of the environment offer a compelling alternative explanation. Thus, the possibility for genetic influences must remain open, and the debate will not soon be put to rest.

Beyond the racist implications of genetically based theories of group differences in intelligence, the pedagogical and social consequences are serious. If certain groups are genetically inferior, then the problem lies not with society but with those groups, and, of course, there is no sense addressing the problem since little can be done to alter genetics. Clearly, this is an over-simplification, however, since there is always a complex interaction between heredity and the environment.

In summary, genetically based theories for the academic under-achievement and social problems associated with certain ethnic groups tend to be opposed by the vast majority of scholars who view such a position as racist and as empirically unfounded. However, the persistence of group differences and the lack of a truly compelling alternative explanation ensure that genetically based theories will not be easily put to rest.

Where Are the Environmentalists?

There is one aspect to the intellectual war over a genetic versus environmental explanation for group differences that disturbs me. For the most part, genetic theorists present their arguments in a methodical and rational manner designed to lend as much scientific credence to their conclusions as possible. Scientists who are outraged by the notion of inherited group inferiority, hoping to deconstruct the genetic argument, respond immediately and emotionally, which only serves to weaken their argument. I recall the privilege of sitting with a small group of senior social scientists immediately following the publication of Jensen's article on race and IQ. The group I was with was naturally outraged, and after some discussion, I, as the junior scientist, offered what I thought was the constructive opinion that, "Well, at least the Jensen article will stimulate a lot of research." The response from one of the senior scientists was, "Yeah, a lot of bad research." His point was that research designed to prove the preeminence of environment over genetics would produce emotionally driven, poorly conceived, and hastily designed experiments.

The result of this form of "gut" reaction to genetic theories is precisely what ensures that the debate will continue. As I noted, social scientists are quick to berate genetic theories, and they feel that all they need do is point to the methodological weaknesses of genetic research. What is lacking, of course, are competing cultural, or more broadly, environmental theories to counteract the genetic position. Simply put, deconstructing genetic theory is half the mission; the other, bigger, half is constructing an environmental theory with hard data. All deconstructing does is drive genetic theorists back to the laboratory to counteract criticism.

Let me illustrate the point. One of the first criticisms leveled at genetic theorists was that so-called IQ tests were culturally biased in favor of Whites. This was a compelling argument and quickly convinced people that African America-White differences on IQ tests were spurious, which only led genetic theorists back to a more careful analysis of the data. They argued that if the tests were biased, we would expect low-scoring Whites to get difficult items on the test wrong, but low-scoring African American should get a different constellation of items wrong. Why? Because it is not African American students lack of ability but lack of cultural knowledge that produces poor performance. The analysis showed clearly that test items that Whites found easy, African Americans also found easy, and both groups had difficulty with the same items. So how can the test be culturally biased?

As argument and counterargument about the cultural biases of test items continued, critics, perhaps feeling beaten down, shifted their attention to motivation. The argument was that, perhaps African American students did less well on IQ tests because they were simply less motivated to perform well. Genetic theorists reacted by analyzing test scores further to come up with a counterargument. They noted that while Whites outperform African Americans on tests generally, there are, nevertheless, a few items where African Americans not only equal but actually outperform Whites. It turns out that one of these items occurs adjacent in the test to an item where Whites outperform African Americans. Are we to believe that African American students are not motivated, but all of a sudden, on one particular item, they become motivated?

My point here is that environmentalists keep pointing to the weaknesses, which only drives genetic theorists to do more research to address the criticisms. To make matters worse, current forms of genetic explanations for group-based differences appear far less racist. This is because comparisons are now made between Asians, Whites, and African Americans, and Asians outperform Whites. How can genetic theories be motivated by racism when Whites do not come out on top?

I want to know where the proactive environmental theorists are? Up until a few years ago, my harangue would end here with a challenge to environmental theorists. But the publication of a seminal book by Jared Diamond, (1997) entitled *Guns, Germs, and Steel*, offers a detailed and compelling argument for an environmentalist interpretation of group differences in development. His is a sweeping and detailed analysis beginning with the observation that, "Peoples of Eurasian origin, especially those still living in Europe and eastern Asia, plus those transplanted to North America, dominate the world in wealth and power. Other peoples, including most Africans, have thrown off European colonial domination but remain far behind in wealth and power. Still other peoples, such as the aboriginal inhabitants of Australia, the Americas, and southernmost Africa, are no longer even masters of their own lands but have been decimated, subjugated, and in some cases even exterminated by European colonialists" (p. 15). Diamond wants to know why Aboriginal Americans, Africans, and Aboriginal Australians did not come to dominate the world.

The simple genetic answer, that it was the most intelligent groups that advanced, leaving the less able behind, is what Diamond sets out to challenge. Diamond's proactive environmental argument begins with what he calls "farmer power." He traces human development from its very beginnings and notes that when humans were nomadic hunters and gatherers, social units were small and every member of the unit performed the same duties leading to relative egalitarianism. The domestication of wild plants and animals revolutionizes human structure. Farming means the social unit lives in one place, allowing for more children to be born, thereby leading to larger social units. Overproduction allows for role specification such that it is now possible to have a full-time leader and full-time warriors. Clearly, such farming groups will have superior power and come to dominate those groups that remain nomadic.

Now comes the crucial question. Why did some groups evolve into farmers quicker than others? The tempting answer is that some peoples are more intelligent than others, our classic genetic argument. Diamond's thesis is that it was strictly a favorable environment that allowed one group to domesticate plants and animals quicker than another. And his evidence is detailed and compelling. For example, he details how, in the form of a natural experiment, a genetically similar group dispersed itself across a series of South Sea Islands with very different environmental conditions. He then proceeds to show how each island, unique in its configuration of terrain, wild plants, sea life, and animals, came to determine a very different social evolution. Similarly, he explains why Aboriginal peoples in North America faced very different ecological challenges from those elsewhere, leading to a clear prediction in terms of social evolution. In this manner, Diamond offers a thoroughly proactive account that leads to an environmental, rather than genetic, explanation for group-based differences in what we have come to call human progress. I can only hope that the present book makes a minor contribution to a proactive environmentalist argument.

Cultural Deficit Theories

Discomfort with genetically based theories soon gave way to what appeared on the surface to be a more socially appropriate explanation of group differences: cultural deficit theory. The basic idea was that groups were equal in terms of inherited intelligence, but certain groups performed poorly in school specifically and in its associated benefits generally because their culture did not provide an environment that was supportive of academic performance. The deficit feature arises because it was argued that certain cultures are not merely different but negligent. Indeed, it was such thinking that formed the theoretical basis of the American war on poverty initiated in the mid-1960s. Youngsters were placed in special pre-school "head-start" programs with the hope that, by the time they entered school, such culturally deprived children would now be able to compete effectively in school. Clearly, the families of these children were judged to be culturally deficient and, thus, their children had to be pulled out of the family for early remedial training and/or their parents needed cultural training in order to provide their children with an environment that was more conducive to learning. The specific "deficits" attributed to these families was that they did not expose their children to an environment that was sufficiently rich in stimulation. Such an analysis is, of course, sheer nonsense, because there is nothing more stimulating than a poor family where there are lots of children and the homes are small. So, stimulus deprivation gave way to deficits about books and reading and supervised instruction and discipline and one-on-one attention.

It was thought initially that a cultural deficit explanation was socially constructive. If a deficient culture was the enemy, then at least groups could be convinced or compelled to change their culture in "appropriate" ways and thereby raise the academic achievement levels of students. Lost in this enthusiasm was the fact that responsibility was placed squarely on the shoulders of minority groups, thus absolving mainstream society of any role in the problem. Blaming the victim was the order of the day.

Proponents of cultural deficit theory naturally endorse a political, social, and pedagogical policy of cultural assimilation, firmly believing that such a policy is in the best interests of minority students. The presumption is that Euro-North American culture and language (English, French) represents the high-status ideal. Requiring groups whose members bear the burden of a deficient culture and language to assimilate to this ideal was deemed to be a generous offering to minority group members. It was an opportunity that would put them on an equal footing with those who were fortunate enough to represent mainstream culture.

Cultural Difference Theory

Cultural deficit theories have given way to a more egalitarian view that emphasizes cultural relativity or cultural "discontinuity." That is, for minority students there is a discontinuity between the culture of home (heritage culture) and the culture of school (mainstream culture). The discontinuity argument still focuses on cultural differences, but the emphasis has shifted from cultural "deficit" to cultural "difference."

The cultural difference explanation for the academic underachievement of minority students is appealing in two important respects. First, it appears to be egalitarian in terms of culture, so that crises of identity for minority students arise out of a genuine competition between two very different cultures that are respected equally. No one is to blame, therefore, for the underachievement that is associated with resolving the resultant confusion over identity.

The second appeal is that it appears to give minority communities some control over the resolution of competing cultures. Because both the heritage and mainstream culture are judged equally, it presupposes that any combination of cultures can be chosen as the basis for identity.

Cultural difference theories are predicated on the assumption that it is possible to articulate the essential values and behavior patterns of a culture. Indeed, research has been directed at specifying the differences between particular cultures, and despite some theorists who deny the existence of fundamental cultural differences, most researchers in the field have been able to describe differences among cultural groups. The result, as it applies to Aboriginal people in the context of education, for example, is a series of values that are proposed to distinguish mainstream culture from Aboriginal culture. These are summarized in Table 4.1.

The value differences depicted in Table 4.1 refer to "White values" and "Indian values." However, many of the same differences have been noted with respect to Inuit culture, and, indeed, Crago and Eriks-Brophy (1993) have documented important aspects of these differences. They have shown how, in Inuit homes, socialization for communicative interaction differs from the patterns of talking to, and with, children that have been documented for mainstream families. Specifically, compared with mainstream "motherese," Inuit mothers spend little time in direct conversation with their children, and children are discouraged from participating in conversations with adults. Questions to which adults know the answers are rarely asked of children, nor are children encouraged to ask questions. Moreover, parents do not typically engage in labeling routines with their children. In short, talkativeness on the part of the child in adult company is viewed as undisciplined behavior.

Clearly, the pattern of interaction described by Crago is highly discontinuous with what is valued in a mainstream classroom. The highly prized verbal behavior of the classroom is completely at odds with Aboriginal cultures where observational learning is so valued. And the rationale for these cultural differences is intuitively obvious. The harsh realities of Artic life leaves no

Table 4.1
Culture Differences Between Indian and White Values

Indian Values	White Values
Group emphasis	Individual emphasis
Cooperation (group concern)	Competition (self-concern)
Present oriented	Future oriented
Non-awareness of time	Awareness of time
Age	Youth
Harmony with nature	Conquest of nature
Giving	Saving
Practical	Theoretical
Patience	Impatience
Extended family	Immediate family
Non-materialistic	Materialistic
Modest	Overstates (over confident)
Silent	Noisy
Low self-value	Strong self-value
Respects other religions	Converts others to own religion
Religion a way of life	Religion a segment of life
Land, water, forests and other resources belong to all, and are used reasonably	Land, water, forests and other resources belong to the private domain, and are use in a greedy manner
Equality	Wealth
Face-to-face government	Representative democracy

Source: Tanner, A. (ed.), 1983, pp. 296–297.

room for error. Education in such a real setting requires the young person to engage in external observations before engaging in survival activities. There is no room for trial-and-error learning that is the hallmark of the modern classroom.

Anyone involved with Aboriginal education will recognize the cultural differences described here, and it would be tempting to conclude that every group will have its own culture that will be more or less discontinuous from that required for success in mainstream formal education. When I first began working in Aboriginal communities, it was an instant déjà vu experience. I had witnessed the same pattern of childrearing in countries like the

Philippines and rural India. Here, I am referring specifically to parents in developing countries socializing their children by having them observe and model at their own pace. Again, this is in marked contrast to the mainstream North American culture with its emphasis on verbal functioning and competition to have children master tasks and become independent.

One is sometimes tempted to propose a simple dichotomy: western culture versus other cultures. Think of the expression so often used by westerners when they are in an "other" culture and events seem to unfold slowly with apparent disregard for scheduling and deadlines: "We must be operating on ——— time." The blank can be filled in with a wide variety of cultural groups, suggesting that those may indeed be common features to what appear to be vastly different cultures.

In summary, cultural difference explanations for the identity confusion that leads to academic underachievement are compelling. Moreover, they are socially desirable because of the respect that is implied for heritage cultures. What is not acknowledged, however, are the dramatic power differences associated with the competing cultures.

Resolving Theoretical Differences

Whether the focus is on genetic, deficit, or difference theories, the common theme is that ethnic groups have their own culture and that culture may be discontinuous with mainstream culture. All three theoretical orientations agree that cultural differences are pivotal, with disagreements centering on why. But even genetically based theorists agree that genetics is only part of the basis of, for example, human intelligence. Moreover, genes are themselves constantly evolving, albeit slowly, in response to the environment. Thus, even if some portion of culture is genetically determined, the argument that, because of genetic inferiority, there is no need to address the academic difficulties of certain ethnic groups is untenable. First, change is possible, and second, who says that "mainstream" institutions should not be required to change in order to accommodate other cultures?

Deficit and difference theories are intellectually identical, differing only in their explicit value judgment. Both agree that cultural differences exist, and both agree that the minority culture may be incompatible with mainstream culture. Thus, we can safely assume that different groups have different cultures and, further, that the closer a minority culture is to "mainstream" Euro–North American culture, the easier the integration process. For example, Heath (1983) notes that in Chinese American families, the style of parent-child interaction parallels that found in mainstream classrooms. Parents ask children factual questions and monitor children's responses by correction and elaboration. Not surprisingly, Chinese American students bring to school a heritage culture that is conducive to performing well in school.

Our concern, however, is with groups who have a disproportionate experience with school failure. Do we need to explore in detail the unique culture of every cultural group with a view to specifying those aspects that might be incompatible with mainstream school culture? I believe our task is not so daunting, but I fear that my conclusion may tread on some cultural toes. Just as individuals are threatened when they are treated as faceless numbers rather than as unique human beings, so, too, cultural groups are threatened when they are lumped with other groups. Scientists, too, are reluctant to believe that communities they work in are not unique. I must confess to some of these same feelings, and yet I am compelled to conclude that there is a remarkable similarity to certain cultural features of all groups who have difficulty with mainstream formal education.

Therefore, I want to lump together all those groups who have difficulty with formal schooling—groups as disparate as the Inuit, the Cree, the Cherokee, Puerto Ricans, African Americans, and Mexican Americans. This array of groups does not share the same color, region, religion, history, or language. Yet I believe they do share certain cultural characteristics that are discontinuous with mainstream formal education.

Key Cultural Differences

We have already described certain characteristics shared by these groups but not what we would normally call "cultural" characteristics. That is, they all have difficulty with formal, Euro–North American schooling. As well, they suffer a similar array of social, economic, and mental health problems.

But what cultural characteristics do they share? This brings us to a fundamental dilemma when it comes to analyzing cultural similarities and differences. Are the superficial differences a reflection of more important and fundamental differences? And, once you have adjusted to the striking differences, do not the similarities seem even more profound? Any sojourner to the communities we are contemplating will be required to integrate a kaleidoscope of superficial differences to middle-class mainstream communities, but our sojourner will be shocked equally by the similarities. The case of Aboriginal people living in isolated Arctic communities is for me one of the best examples of the simultaneous impression of difference and similarity. Being above the tree line, the land is stark and the village constitutes a collection of identical square boxes, colorfully and symmetrically built according to some mainstream southern urban planner rather than the natural environment. Hydroelectric poles and communication lines dominate the community since there are no trees to disguise their symmetrical ugliness. For the same reason, every minute piece of garbage stands out. And movement about the village is dominated by trucks, all-terrain vehicles, and skidoos, driven by everyone from six-year-olds on up. A visitor can only marvel at the number of people that can be transported by a small, four-wheeled vehicle and why only occasionally people use the few designated roads in the village.

The people look different and sound different, and children are everywhere. There are children inside and outside and at every adult gathering, reminding you of the statistic that, in Arctic Quebec, over 50 percent of the population is under the age of 15! But for all the children, and as young as they are, there is very little fuss and crying. Why? Because babies are not transported in sterile, mechanical carriages held at arm's length by some suspicious parent worried that the streets and the mall are unsafe environments for the young. Instead, in Aboriginal communities, babies go everywhere, are tended by anyone, and are always carried in adult clothing so that there is constant human contact.

But with all the striking differences, there is an equally striking similarity. The school looks like any school in a middle-class urban community. The office and classroom configurations are identical and the mandatory gymnasium, which doubles as the venue for all social events and meetings, looks very familiar. And there is the familiar yellow bus picking up the children even in a community of 300 people, where the longest walk to school would be less than a city block.

The point of my digression is to underline the challenge involved in specifying cultural differences that are truly profound differences. Our observations of superficial aspects of community life point to striking differences and equally striking similarities. At a more profound level, we need to specify which values, personality characteristics, or cognitive styles are genuinely different from so-called mainstream characteristics.

The challenge can be illustrated succinctly by focusing on a characteristic that is judged to be profound and frustrating to mainstreamers—time. While mainstreamers are driven by schedules and punctuality, the groups we are focusing on seem oblivious to time. Is this a genuine cultural difference, or does it reflect a more profound lack of motivation that makes adherence to some Euro–North American preordained schedule irrelevant?

In my search for cultural differences that are important, I engage Aboriginal students in the exercise I described in another chapter. The exercise is designed to reveal essential cultural components, and I begin by asking, what is unique about your culture? The answers I receive usually focus on visible aspects of culture such as ceremonies, foods, clothing, and sometimes language. I then pose a series of questions about these aspects of culture in the form of, "If you didn't participate in such and such a ceremony, would you still be a ———?" The answer is always an immediate "yes," except that when I ask about their heritage language there is always some hesitation followed by a reluctant admittance that they would still be Inuit or Cree even if they no longer spoke their language.

This exercise always leads to a discussion of fundamental value differences between their group and Euro–North American culture, which leaves us all baffled. For example, people will say, "We value sharing" and my first thought is always, "But that's a value I was taught from the cradle." I then conclude that maybe there are no value differences, it is just that my culture is not very good at acting in a way that is consistent with the value.

The Reality of Cultural Differences

It may seem that I am leading to the conclusion that there are no cultural differences, at least profound ones, but I am not. I do believe there are cultural differences, but I also believe we have to return to the fundamental question of what culture is, the question that we addressed in Chapter 3.

Definitions vary from shared values and attitudes to behavior (ways of doing things) to language and the extent to which it may shape thought to shared personality characteristics, to cognitive styles to a shared history. With so many definitions, it is clear that "culture" is a construct that is difficult to define. Everyone will have a different definition, and I will only add to the confusion by forming my own view.

First, it is clear that cultural differences are more or less obvious depending upon the focus. A fundamental distinction in cross-cultural psychology is between "etics" and "emics." Etics refer to aspects of life that are pancultural or universal. Emics refer to features that are culture specific. Researchers are actively searching for which features are emic and which are etic. My own view is that any feature can be either emic or etic depending upon the level of abstraction. Having feelings is universal, but the subtleties of how these are expressed will be culture specific. Thoughts are universal, but which are practiced more and become finely tuned will be culture specific. Fairness and reciprocity in human relations may be universal, but how these are defined in behavior will be culture specific. Thus, in my view, theorists can argue effectively for or against the reality and importance of cultural differences by conveniently shifting the level at which differences are sought.

I will go further and argue that, all too often, social scientists focus on cute examples of cultural differences as a cover-up for no clear notion of culture and its importance. They enjoy describing how in certain cultures people stand very close to one another when they speak, causing discomfort for those whose culture requires a little more interpersonal space. They delight in pointing out the cultural misunderstandings that can arise. I have experienced numerous of these. For example, I am a person from a culture that preaches that when you are a guest for dinner, "You must finish everything on your plate" as a signal that the meal was delicious. I was a guest in a culture where, as a guest, you should, "Always leave some food on your plate" in order to signal that your host has been so generous that you could not possibly eat all that has been provided. Imagine this scene from Laurel and Hardy, to say nothing of my embarrassed hosts and my expanded waistline. Fortunately, a later discussion of cultural differences left us all closer for the experience. And, finally, in terms of underachievement, it has been noted that in certain cultures it is inappropriate to make eye contact when being addressed by an authority (for example, a teacher) whereas in other cultures, eye contact is a sign that the message is being listened to seriously.

As real as these differences are, I am hard pressed to believe that they are profound and that people do not very quickly learn what I would deem to be superficial cultural differences. Culture is socially constructed, not something that is innately determined. What is being suggested here is that a group's ecological and social reality will lead members of that group to evolve effective culture-specific ways of maximizing their management of social and ecological reality. No doubt cultures that have evolved in the context of an ever-changing physical environment, as confronts those who live in arctic or desert conditions, will develop a highly developed sense of spatial relations. But does this mean that, if exposed to a different social and ecological environment, these same people are incapable of developing other skills? I find that hard to believe.

We are left with two puzzling questions that must be resolved. First, if culture is so important that people are willing to die in order to protect it, why is it so difficult to define? Second, if culture is socially constructed, then why can cultures not evolve in order to meet a group's new challenges? Putting the questions in terms of the challenge of the present volume, "What profound cultural characteristics do groups who experience academic underachievement bring to the school environment, and why can they not alter certain aspects of their culture so as to become more successful in school?"

I do believe that cultural characteristics are profound, and I believe that they lead to a fundamental mismatch with Euro–North American culture. Moreover, I believe that these cultural differences manifest themselves in every social domain, but nowhere is it more visible than in formal education, the one institution that is shared by members of every group.

First, I believe that there are cultural differences in child socialization and that the groups we are emphasizing, Euro–North American groups, on the one hand, and Aboriginal people, African American, Mexican American, Puerto Rican, and many traditional developing countries, on the other, lie at opposite poles of the contrast. Euro-North American parents actively engage their children to learn and emphasize early mastery, and while this is a general style, it is especially directed at skills that are consistent with formal schooling. Contrasting cultures tend to have their children learn by sharing the environment with adults and by having children observe them performing every conceivable task. No emphasis is placed on early mastery or on skills associated with formal education since members of the groups we are addressing do not have much experience themselves with formal education or its antecedent conditions.

The result of this profound cultural difference is an orientation to formal schooling that is a complete mismatch with what is required to succeed. Children are not comfortable with abstract thought, having been raised to observe the concrete and to derive meaning from context. As well, children do not tend to link present behavior with long-term projections, again because such links are not obvious in observational learning. Indeed, Euro-North American parents spend countless hours trying to explain to even very young children that proficiency in reading will have positive, if not easily identifiable, adult consequences.

My conclusions about these cultural differences are not merely rooted in my own idiosyncratic observations. Psychologists and anthropologists have empirically researched the issue far better than I. However, I am anything but confident when it comes to articulating cultural differences and our understanding of them. Take the recurring theme that certain cultural groups have little respect for time, cannot delay gratification, and are not oriented to directly teaching. I remember as a graduate student reading a social scientist's account of how these cultural characteristics apply to the particular group he was analyzing. My eyes rolled back in my head when, in the same paragraph, he noted that the group's penchant for having lots of children was so the parents would have people to take over the farm when they became old and feeble. If that is not planning ahead, what is?

Cultural Differences and Collective Identity

In Chapter 3, I argued that collective identity is the most important psychological construct for healthy adjustment and that, of all a person's collective identities, none is more central than cultural identity. We can appreciate the challenge faced by members of severely disadvantaged groups who are forced to integrate two collective identities that are fundamentally contradictory. The challenge is particularly problematic because the collective identities involved are cultural identities. Cultural identity is the one that touches every domain of human functioning, and so it is not simply that the individual can integrate the two collective identities by keeping both but applying one in a home and community context and the other in a school and work context. Because the collective identities in question are cultural, nothing short of a complete integration will suffice.

As challenging as integrating discontinuous cultures is, it cannot on its own explain the profound malaise that characterizes profoundly disadvantaged groups. As we detailed in Chapter 2, examples abound of racially and culturally different minority groups who are highly successful in North American society. With this in mind, we turn our attention in the next chapter to the issue of not merely cultural differences but cultural power differences, in short, colonialism.

CHAPTER 5

Valueless Colonialism and the Destruction of Collective Identity

My review of cultural difference theories leads to the conclusion that disadvantaged minority groups are faced with the challenge of integrating two incompatible collective identities. Clearly, there is more to the story than the resolution of cultural differences. As we learned in Chapter 2, some groups are apparently very successful at reconciling competing collective identities; others, those that are the focus of the present volume, are far less successful. How can we account for this fundamental difference?

I propose that the power differential between the competing collective identities is what makes the reconciling of collective identities so problematic. When one cultural group has complete power over another, the task of integrating the powerful collective identity with the much less powerful heritage collective identity is overwhelming. To begin with, the whole motivation to do so is lacking. After all, the less powerful group does not voluntarily choose to place itself in a bicultural context: it's imposed on them. By contrast, groups that are more successful at integrating competing cultural identities choose to expose themselves to that challenge. Presumably, they do so, first, because they believe that the competing culture will be a constructive addition to their collective identity and, second, because they are confident they can achieve an integrated collective identity. Groups that are overpowered by another cultural group do not choose to incorporate the new powerful collective identity and therefore are not motivated to engage the process and probably have little confidence in the possibility for constructive resolution. This point has been argued most cogently by Ogbu and Matute-Bianchi (1986).

Colonialism theories are explicit in attempting to explain group-based academic underachievement and social problems as resulting from collective identity differences, where emphasis is placed on the differential power between the cultural groups. Frideres (1988) is an articulate proponent of colonialism theory as it applies to Aboriginal people. He describes "the Indian reserve as an internal colony that is exploited by the dominant White group in Canada. White Canadians are seen as the colonizing people while Natives are considered the colonized people" (p. 366).

Colonialism, in its traditional form, refers to unequal relations involving a "mother country" that exploits the labor power or natural resources of an external "subject country" or colony. Classic examples include European "mother countries" that have colonized countries in Asia, Latin America, and Africa.

Colonial relations are not limited to different nations but can exist within a single nation and, hence, the introduction of the concept of "internal colonialism" to refer to those situations where colonizing nations have settled in new lands and have subjugated both indigenous and non-indigenous groups. The classic case of internal colonialism is the United States and relations between white Europeans and African Americans; however, internal colonialism models have been applied frequently to Aboriginal people.

Frideres (1988) has applied internal colonialism to the Canadian context by elaborating six components to the process:

1. The incursion of the colonizing group into a geographical area.
2. The destruction of the social and cultural structures of Aboriginal peoples.
3. The establishment of political control over Aboriginal peoples.
4. Forcing Aboriginal peoples into a state of economic dependence.
5. Inadequate social services.
6. Institutional and interpersonal racism.

The devastating impact of the differential cultural power associated with colonialism cannot be overestimated. African Americans did not ask to be kidnapped and sold into slavery thousands of miles away. Aboriginal people did not invite Europeans to come and force them onto reserves. Mexican Americans did not anticipate having to illegally scrape a living off land they once owned, and Puerto Ricans had barely begun to cope with the intrusion of Spanish culture when the United States imposed its culture.

And what of the sheer magnitude of the cultural devastation? It has been suggested that European colonizers caused the death of a staggering 100 million Aboriginal people in the Americas. Eleven million Africans were transported for sale in the New World, to say nothing of those who did not survive the voyage.

And what was the fate of those who actually survived? Like most privileged members of North American society, I have come to learn about the impact of colonialism from eloquent people who have experienced colonialism firsthand. I often found these personal testimonies to involve such inhumanity that I honestly believe I coped by denying their reality. But what I cannot deny is the reality of all those Aboriginal friends and colleagues who have shared with me their most intimate experiences. Cataloguing their experiences would minimize them, so let me limit my comments to two simple observations. I have not met one Aboriginal person over the age of 40 who was not beaten repeatedly for speaking his or her heritage language within earshot of their colonizer teachers. In a totally different context, I remember being stunned when an African American colleague remembered, as we drove across the causeway to Miami Beach, "When I was growing up we were not allowed to go to Miami Beach unless we had an identity card indicating we were domestic servants."

These are obvious examples, but so many times I have needed people to point out for me the less visible examples of cultural destruction. It took a geographer to point out that all the roads in Mozambique run from the hinterland to the coast, with no inland connectors. The simple reason was that Portuguese colonizers were only interested in an infrastructure that would allow them to transport goods from inland to their ships in the harbor.

Let me share another example that on the surface seems benign but illustrates how cultural power threatens heritage cultures. Picture a remote Inuit village from an airplane. High in the endless, treeless expanse of tundra lies a cluster of brightly painted houses clinging to the rock overlooking the frozen bay. There may be 50 houses at most, with two larger buildings drawing the focus of attention: the skating arena and the school. There are only one or two little roads winding through the village, and they extend only a few kilometers outside the village, one to the dump, the other to the airport. Below, a collection of 150 adults and at least as many children under the age of 15 pursue a lifestyle that most mainstream North Americans have only read about.

Despite their remoteness, this small collection of Inuit has not escaped the worst devastation that colonialism reeked upon all Aboriginal peoples in North America. Indeed, the very existence of a settled village is testimony to the ravages of colonialism. After all, the Inuit traditionally moved in small extended families with the seasons, ever in search of the elusive fish and game that determined their very survival. It was White bureaucrats, unable to fully control such unpredictable mobility, who forced Inuit families together, decided where they would live permanently, and designed the housing that would replace their chosen way of life.

But these are different times; empowerment has come to Aboriginal communities and with it a sense that Aboriginal people have some control over their own destiny. What is the reality? Without question, Aboriginal people are recapturing a lost identity and in many cases revitalizing their heritage language. Traditional values and lifestyle are celebrated and, indeed, to some extent incorporated formally into the classroom. On the other hand, the impact of mainstream society is pervasive: Modern technology is in evidence everywhere, even in a remote Inuit village. One striking example are the hydroelectric poles and wires that dominate the village, because there are no trees at this latitude to disguise their ugliness. The school itself is a mainstream institution, and it looks frighteningly like every other school in North America with a front office buzzing with telephones, fax machines, and computers. The classrooms look familiar and were it not for the distinctive Aboriginal pictures and heritage language symbols adorning the walls, one could easily be in Toronto, Chicago, or Los Angeles.

But these represent only the obvious remnants of colonialism. More accurately in today's climate perhaps they represent the unintended power of mainstream culture to impact every corner of the country. I do not fear such obvious displays of cultural power. Well, yes I do fear such cultural power, but at least its visibility places Aboriginal people in a position to recognize its impact on the community and to choose whether or not to embrace it.

My foci here, however, are the small, rarely noticed examples of cultural imperialism that may in the end be life threatening, or at least culture threatening, from an Inuit perspective. My examples are all the more poignant, because my first reaction to them was innocent laughter. It was only later, and upon reflection, that their enormity struck me.

The examples are trivial at first glance. The first involves a bright yellow school bus. The bus is identical to the thousands that adorn every mainstream community, replete with flashing red lights and extended arm with a giant "stop" sign. Normally, a school bus would not attract any undue attention, save for one startling fact. Why on earth does a community need a school bus when the farthest a child might live from the school is no more than one city block?

The second example involves the practice of choosing two members of the community, who live at opposite ends of the village, to serve as storm watchers. Their task is to evaluate weather conditions and ultimately decide whether classes need to be canceled.

I told you the examples were trivial, and when first confronted with them, I was somewhat curious and somewhat more amused. But upon reflection, it was my amusement that I focused on. Why was I amused? In the case of the bus, it seemed bizarre to have a bus in a tiny village where any student could walk to school quicker than travel by bus. Canceling school because of a snowstorm barely makes sense in a southern urban environment, but not for Inuit whose adaptation to winter conditions is legendary.

The tragedy dawns upon reflection of my amusement. Inuit have had their heritage culture shattered by colonialism. That any trace of their culture remains is testimony to their collective will. And that will has received an impetus with a new age of empowerment, a gradual devolution of power to Aboriginal peoples everywhere, including the Inuit. The result has been concerted attempts to make formal education culturally relevant, to revive heritage languages in some cases and protect them in others, and, ultimately, to move toward self-government.

Surely the bus and storm watch vignettes are trivial in the context of such fundamental concerns. I do not think so. Essentially, the village has a bus because all southern schools have buses, and the storm watchers are a local adaptation to southern school board procedures where decisions about school cancellations due to weather are formalized. So far, no serious problem. But at the very heart of Inuit identity is a legacy of adapting to the harshest environment on the planet. Every cultural value finds its roots in the Inuit capacity to survive. Everything from their nomadic lifestyle to their profound emphasis on sharing spring from their ingenuity and will to survive.

Mainstream visitors to the North are incredulous at the ease with which Inuit interface with their environment. I have on numerous occasions found myself completely lost a mere three kilometers from a village. The usual anchor points are absent: no human-built structures, no trees, only a seemingly endless undulation of rock and ponds. And even so close to the village, with no clue as to the direction home, it occurs to you that you could never survive long in this driving wind and cold. Inuit do not get it. They move gracefully for miles across the tundra, always with quiet certainty and pride.

Back to our bus and storm watch exercise. Both involve borrowing practices initiated in a southern, urban environment. Even here this rationale is dubious, but clearly neither makes much sense in the North. If transplanting these peripheral mainstream education practices to the North were the extent of the problem, they would merely represent one more superficial indication of the cultural power of mainstream culture. But in the case of the bus and the storm watchers, the transplant threatens the very core of

Inuit identity: the ability to adapt to a harsh environment. Young children are being robbed of that identity when they are loaded on a yellow bus instead of making the short walk to school. It affects how they dress, the ease with which they habituate themselves to the environment, and indeed, it challenges the very physical and mental toughness that such habituation requires.

This threat to cultural identity, both symbolic and real, is exacerbated by the storm watchers. Surely, Inuit children should be in a position to express pride were they in a position to say to their mainstream counterparts from the South, "Cancel school because of a snow storm? Don't be ridiculous, we're not babies." I have often spoken with such pride myself when, as a resident of a Canadian city, I have spoken to colleagues from sunny California, whom I secretly envy, but instead disguise by expressing my Canadian identity. If it works for me, Inuit have to be the world champions. And lest anyone feels I am being too harsh on Inuit children, let me hasten to assure you that anytime school is canceled because of a storm, it never stops the children from running around the village having a great time. Come to think of it, that in itself is evidence of their adaptability. Let us not symbolically rob them of it with yellow buses and storm watches.

There are two features of the cultural power differential associated with colonialism that need to be underscored. First, members of colonized groups did not choose to expose themselves to a new culture, and, second, the status of the heritage culture is squashed under the weight of the culture of the colonizer.

Immigrants to North America have chosen to expose themselves to a new culture. Moreover, as I have noted, North America receives only a select few from any particular ethnic group: usually those that are talented and highly motivated. Even refugees, whose desperate situation in their home country has forced them to leave, at least have a small degree of choice in terms of what culture they choose to expose themselves to. Colonization forces a new culture not just on a select few but indiscriminately on all members of a colonized group. And, whereas immigrant groups may experience a degree of racism or more accurately ethnicism, in the case of colonized groups, the power differential ensures the complete degradation of the colonized culture.

What needs to be appreciated is the extent to which the cultural power differential associated with colonialism dislocates every corner of the colonized group's heritage culture. Oversimplified analyses of colonialism allude to the three "Ms:" military, missionaries, and merchants. In terms of the military, it is clear that the intention is entirely exploitive. But missionaries were often well intentioned, and merchants were merely trying to "cut the best business deal," a practice they would engage in with any person or group they might trade with. Whether the motivation of colonizers is constructive or destructive, it is the power differential that ultimately destroys the heritage culture.

Even a cursory examination of the effects of colonization on the culture of Aboriginal people illustrates the extent to which their collective identity has been destroyed. Colonization meant that groups that were largely nomadic, roaming in small extended family collectives, were forced to live sedentary lives either on bounded land-poor reserves, in the case of North American Indians, or in fixed communities, in the case of Inuit. Formal schooling and commerce forced families apart. In the case of schooling, it meant removing children from their family for a good portion of the day or, worse, sending children to schools thousands of miles away, which meant they were separated from their families for months at a time. Meantime, the ravages of new diseases and the mixed blessings associated with new technology, if nothing else radically changed the lifestyle of Aboriginal people.

I have refrained from a lengthy digression into the inhuman treatment that colonized peoples suffered. My restraint is based on the desire to focus for the moment on how the heritage culture of colonized groups was irrefutably damaged. When cultural difference theorists point to severely disadvantaged groups as facing the challenge of integrating two equal cultures, they minimize the challenge. What differential power necessitates is the integration of two cultures where one of the cultures has been severely fractured.

COLONIALISM AND HERITAGE LANGUAGES

One of the best illustrations of the profound impact of the power associated with colonialism is the domain of language. Specifically, in the growing debate over bilingual education, intergroup power is pivotal. The pedagogical challenge, which initially gave rise to bilingual forms of education, was how to help minority children, whose home language was not English, compete effectively in the school environment. Because the problem was initially framed in purely language terms, the solution was simple: Submerse minority language children in English as quickly as possible and for as long as possible. The aim was to maximize the chances that the child would perform well in a school and in a society that functions exclusively in English.

This form of language submersion was so unsuccessful that new solutions were sought. What emerged from the ineffectiveness of submersion, and partly as a response to legislation in the United States that not to be sensitive to the home language of minority children was discriminatory (*Lau v. Nichols*, 1974), were "transitional" forms of bilingualism. Minority students would be taught in their home language for the first two or three years of their education, and then they would be transitioned into an all English curriculum for the remainder of their schooling. Alternatively, minority students would be given some of their schooling in the home language until such time that their English skills were sufficient to permit them to function in the regular English stream. Transitional bilingual programs, therefore, involve using the home language in order to help minority children ultimately participate in a regular mainstream English curriculum.

It may seem that transitional bilingualism is an enlightened form of education that shows concrete respect for heritage languages. But let us look a little closer. First, transitional programs are designed to help minority students assimilate to English, not to convey any respect for the heritage language. For example, here is how transitional bilingualism works. Suppose a child from Portugal with very little English fluency enrolls in a school located in a major American city. The child will be tested in English and, if found lacking, will be stigmatized as an LEP (Limited English Proficiency) student. The child, so stigmatized, will be pulled from regular classes and given instruction in Portuguese so that he or she will not fall too far behind in terms of course content. At the end of the year, the child will be retested in English and, if minimal standards are met, the child will be mainstreamed in the all-English regular program. The child, of course, still faces potential failure for, after all, she or he has only reached minimal standards in English. The point here is that, even for immigrants to North America, most bilingual programs are fundamentally disrespectful of heritage languages. Moreover, they are designed to almost guarantee academic failure.

But this pales in comparison to the plight of Aboriginal and African American people. Internal colonization has not been merely disrespectful of heritage languages, it has destroyed them. Of 83 Aboriginal groups in Canada, only three have a heritage language that has some hope of survival. And how many African languages do African Americans still speak? Indeed, where does the African American community fit in the context of language, generally, and bilingual education, specifically. Lost is the one-word answer. No wonder there are desperate attempts on the part of the African American community to have its form of the English language, Ebonics, treated like a formal language that is distinct from English. The need is twofold. First, it is surely an attempt to recapture what was lost when their heritage languages were destroyed. Second, declaring Ebonics to be a recognized language would mean that African American students could participate in the resources and degree of respect accorded other language minority students in America.

When a child from an immigrant family, be it Portugal, Italy, or Greece, loses his or her heritage language, that is tragic for the child and the family, but no one believes that Portuguese, Italian, and Greek will be lost as world languages. But when one Aboriginal child loses, or one African American child has lost, his or her language, it spells the death for an entire heritage language and, by extension, a people.

The implications of internal colonialism for collective identity conflict are straightforward. The colonizer ultimately expects those who are colonized to assimilate if they are to participate in society. The expectation, then, is that those to be colonized will divest themselves of their heritage culture and language, and adopt mainstream culture and language to the fullest extent possible.

The conflict in collective identity produced by assimilation in this case is multifaceted. First, it requires giving up a cherished and meaningful set of beliefs, values, and behavior patterns. Second, it requires embracing a culture and language that is desirable in terms of the power it affords those who acquire the elements successfully. But it also involves frustration and loss of esteem when, because of systematic discrimination, those colonized persons who have mastered mainstream culture and language are nevertheless denied the opportunity to participate fully in society.

The Myth of Empowerment

Mainstream society has begun to recognize the powerlessness of disadvantaged groups, and with much good intention has sought ways to "empower" them. If nothing else, the widespread popularity of the label "empowerment" signals a clear recognition that having control over one's destiny is of paramount importance. Disadvantaged groups have embraced the concept with enthusiasm, and mainstream groups are patting themselves on the back for being so righteous and sensitive.

But empowerment is more illusory than real, and nowhere is this more evident than the so-called empowerment of Aboriginal people. The key to empowerment is control and the issue is who has control over whom. How the issue of control has evolved with respect to Aboriginal people and mainstream society is depicted schematically in Figure 5.1.

There are four quadrants to Figure 5.1, and they are designed to follow a counterclockwise sequence. Beginning with the upper left quadrant, the label "self-government" indicates that, clearly, mainstream society has control over its own affairs. The arrow directs us to the lower left quadrant,

Figure 5.1
Schematic Representation of Power Relations Between Mainstream Society and Aboriginal People

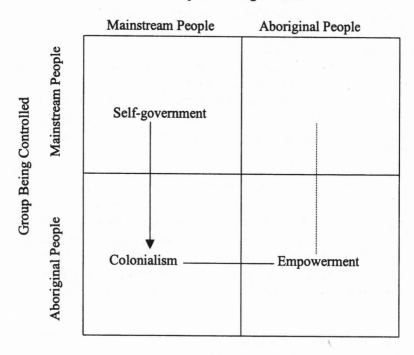

Group Exercising Control

	Mainstream People	Aboriginal People
Mainstream People	Self-government	
Aboriginal People	Colonialism ——————	———— Empowerment

Group Being Controlled

which depicts the traditional colonial relationship where mainstream society had complete control over Aboriginal people. The shift to empowerment occurs in the lower right quadrant where for the first time Aboriginal people have been given some control over their own affairs, but in no sense are we talking full control. The very fact that I have described mainstream society as giving power or control indicates how limited the devolution and power really is. After all, you can only give power if you have it to give. Moreover, even when powers are transferred, they resemble a token gesture. For example, Aboriginal people have been given more control over education, yet they depend on mainstream government for funding.

While mainstream society applauds itself for empowering Aboriginal people, notice that our counterclockwise arrow does not continue to the upper right quadrant. This is the quadrant that indicates that Aboriginal people might have some impact on mainstream society. If Aboriginal people had genuine empowerment, would they not influence mainstream society just as mainstream society has influenced them? I would not expect the mutual influence to be equal, for, after all, there is a large number differential. But the fact that mainstream society does not even pay lip service to mutual influence makes empowerment more illusory than real.

Valueless Colonialism

My own theory is that severely disadvantaged group members are not merely trapped in a conflict of collective identity but that they face the ultimate devastation, a collective identity vacuum. That is, while I endorse theories of cultural differences as they have evolved in the context of internal colonialism, I believe that the crisis in identity is one of both conflict and confusion arising from competing cultures that are devoid of fundamental values. Aboriginal people do not merely face the pushes and pulls of their heritage culture, on the one hand, and mainstream culture, on the other. Rather, they confront a heritage culture that is itself a confusing array of values and practices as a consequence of internal colonialism. Moreover, they have not been exposed to mainstream culture in any clear and systematic way. What has been communicated to Aboriginal people is a confusing model of mainstream culture where certain practices have been emphasized and other fundamental values and practices have been sometimes ignored and in other cases hidden. Colonized people, then, have their identity conflicts compounded by the fact that the two competing cultural identities are themselves poorly defined templates.

In terms of the heritage culture, internal colonialism theories have been explicit in their impact. The process of exploitation and assimilation had the effect, intentionally or unintentionally, of shattering heritage cultures. For example, an Inuit student cannot easily turn to a clearly defined cultural prototype upon which to build an identity. At best, the student must rely on reconstructions of past idealized descriptions of traditional values and ways of life. This is precisely why Aboriginal people in the process of redefining their heritage culture hearken back to precolonial times for a romanticized image of collective identity. Similarly, it is not shocking that the African American community seeks its roots and indeed labels itself in preslavery Africa, a country that most have never visited.

Making Mainstream Culture Incomprehensible

The assumption underlying cultural differences and internal colonialism theories is that, like it or not, Aboriginal people were exposed to a new and powerful culture, that of Western Europe. The fundamentals of European and Aboriginal culture were dramatically different. Historically, Aboriginal people were hunters and gatherers, pursuing a nomadic lifestyle where the pattern of social organization was the extended family. The primary motivations were the arduous challenge of survival and maintaining reproduction rates at or above that of the collectivity. Thus, the search for food was essential and all-consuming.

A recent experience in the metropolis that I call home has given me a new appreciation for the all-consuming nature of survival. A series of three consecutive ice storms brought widespread devastation to the province's hydroelectric system. Concretely, this meant thousands of downed hydro poles, fallen trees, and, for me personally as for hundreds of thousands of others, it meant 17 days without electricity. My days were filled with chopping wood, feeding a fireplace day and night to keep warm, constant trips to the lake for water, and every meal was a major undertaking. I found these minor inconveniences to be so time consuming and exhausting that if I completed any academic work during those 17 days, I felt extremely self-righteous. Upon reflection, I can only marvel at how inhabitants of the Arctic survived, and I have a new appreciation for how all-consuming mere survival must have been.

European culture arose out of an agricultural base that soon involved a social structure that was static rather than nomadic and a social unit that became much larger than the extended family. What emerged was an industrial society characterized by large social structures comprised of specialists who depended upon complex written and verbal language to coordinate the different societal roles. Survival was, for the most part, taken for granted, and attention was turned to the accumulation of material goods, wealth, and power.

These aspects of European culture immediately impacted on Aboriginal cultures. For example, Inuit were encouraged to give up their nomadic lifestyle and their extended family organization. This was accomplished by establishing permanent trading posts where Inuit were now hunting not merely for survival but in order to trade fish and furs. Formal churches and schools were established to encourage people to remain in one settlement year-round. Indeed, the introduction of formal schooling placed Inuit in a hopeless dilemma: On the one hand, they could maintain their nomadic tradition, but this meant leaving their children behind at the school, or they could remain near the school and abandon their nomadic tradition. The point, here, is that only these highly tangible aspects of European culture were visible to Inuit. So, Inuit were only exposed to fragments of European culture, and even these fragments were presented without the benefit of context.

Equally important for our analysis, however, is what was not presented to Aboriginal people in terms of European culture. While Aboriginal people were no doubt overwhelmed by the visible aspects of European culture, they were never exposed to the fundamental values that lie at the core of European culture. These values were not focused on survival but, instead, revolved around the acquisition of material goods. At the heart of European values is *meritocracy*, the notion that a person's status is associated with his or her performance based on ability and effort. As we have noted, Aboriginal people were only exposed to fragments of European culture, and the position Aboriginal people occupied within this fragmented cultural structure was limited to the lowest status positions. Thus, Aboriginal people were offered no opportunity to learn the fundamentals of the European meritocracy. That is, they had no opportunity to learn that they too, based on their ability and effort, could become merchants and teachers if they so desired.

The fragmented image of European culture that was presented to Aboriginal people is particularly striking in the domain of education. Formal education was a fundamental institution for European culture. It was viewed by all as the mechanism by which the individual could acquire the systematic body of knowledge necessary to "get ahead" in European culture. Thus, everyone in European culture shared the belief that formal education was linked directly to success in the job market. It was clear to everyone that the higher the formal education and the better the performance in school, the higher the status of job the individual would attain. The correspondence between formal education and job status was certainly not perfect, but the important point is that those raised in a European culture believed it.

Aboriginal people had European education thrust on them, but they were not provided with a clear understanding of its role and function. Moreover, there was no clear link between formal education and job status. Ironically, this lack of a relationship between job status and education operates in two directions. Most often, even if Aboriginal students complete their formal training, they will not be hired for the job they have been trained for. I remember when in a fit of guilt the government forced White construction companies to make sure that 10 percent of their personnel were Aboriginal. What did the companies do? They hired Aboriginal carpenters and paid them to stay home. Conversely, students who advance beyond high school often do not complete their program because they are persuaded by enormously high salaries to take up a high status position in their home community. Why would salaries be so high? Again, the government pours money into the communities. The issue is not that communities receive financial resources; the problem is the resources have none of the contingencies normally associated with mainstream ideology.

Even within the formal institution of the school, Aboriginal people were not exposed to the fundamentals of European values. The European value of merit is based on the premise that only individual performance based on ability and effort should be rewarded. In the context of school, this means that rewards in the form of marks or grades or promotion should be based solely on performance. What those raised in a European culture understood was that formal education was absolutely necessary, that children, adolescents, and even young adults should pursue formal education as far as they could, which meant as far as their abilities and effort could take them. Further, it was believed that students would be required to "perform" on demand in the form of exams, just as they would be required to perform later on the job. According to the value system, grades on tests were to be assigned on the basis of performance only, and factors such as the student's race, gender, or family connections were not to be influential. It was also understood that not all students would perform at a high enough level to allow them to continue receiving formal education.

Not surprisingly, parents took formal education for their children very seriously and would spend hours helping their children master school material. The value of merit also extended to teachers and administrators; only the most qualified would be hired or promoted.

What we have described here is the idealized form that formal education takes when European values and culture are applied. It must be made clear that not everyone raised in a European culture would have precisely the same understanding of formal education, nor are the principles of "merit" always applied faithfully. Finally, our discussion of western European values as they apply to formal education is not designed to justify them, only to describe them.

When in the process of colonization formal education was introduced to Aboriginal people, most of the key underlying bases for that education were not offered. True, Aboriginal people saw schools being built, teachers being hired, and classes being given. However, nowhere was the fundamental link between education and economic prosperity clearly delineated. At no time were the fundamentals of the value of merit explained or modeled.

Let me offer two more specific examples of how society's most disadvantaged groups have not been socialized in terms of how education really works. My constant companion in an inner-city African American ghetto was a middle-aged lady with seven children she raised on her own. She once announced to me with great excitement that one of her boys was going to be a doctor. In answer to my question, "How do you know?, she responded "Because he is still in school." Further conversation underscored my point here. Her son was in his first year of high school, and unlike her other older children, this son attended school two or three days a week. She had been force-fed and internalized the superficial propaganda that staying in school is important, but she had no real comprehension of what it meant for a young person to be accepted into medical school. She had no realization of the lofty grades that would be needed and the out-of-reach entrance test scores that would enable her son to be one of the select few who gain admission to medical school.

My second example comes from hours of talking with Aboriginal parents who also have internalized the notion that school is important. And this is even as I have described earlier where there is no contingency between education and job prospect. When our conversations revolved around the sporadic attendance of their children at school, it became clear that parents had no idea that school curricula are programmatic. That is, they viewed formal education as the imparting of discrete elements of information to the students so that the learning of one element in no way impacts on learning another. What had never been explained to parents was that what students learn on Monday needs to be mastered before they can understand material presented on Tuesday. No wonder the students do not feel compelled to attend school everyday, and no wonder they find school incomprehensible.

It is always a challenge to pinpoint specific, fundamental attitudes and behaviors that lie at the heart of a cultural mismatch, but I have come to appreciate one fundamental difference that illuminates how society's most disadvantaged have not been exposed to mainstream culture in an honest manner. Traditional Inuit life was literally a struggle to survive, with no margin for error. Food, shelter, and maintaining health were an all day, every day challenge in the harshest climate in the world. Socializing young people was a serious business. Young people learned to hunt, sew, and prepare food by watching and observing and asking questions and practicing. No time for games. No time for adults to ask questions of young people when the adult already knew the answer to the question. No time for trial and error in the learning process, because out on the frozen tundra any mistake might be catastrophic. Only when the young person was deemed "ready" by an elder would a young person come of age by engaging an activity that, hopefully, they had over-learned to maximize their chances for survival.

From this perspective, our formal education seems odd. It is designed to teach by encouraging students to engage in trial and error. Specifically, using a variant of the Socratic method, the teacher poses a question and students compete to guess at the answer. If every student could answer the question correctly, the teacher would judge that the question was too easy and quickly move on to more difficult items. If the student makes a mistake, the consequences are trivial. Well, to be fair, it may not seem trivial to a student who feels inadequate after offering a wrong answer, but the teacher will constantly encourage students to attempt an answer underscoring that there is no shame in failure. The idea is that students are encouraged to acquire information in the protected environment of the school where mistakes are not costly. The hope is that, through this process, the student will accumulate skills so that when he or she graduates to the "real" world mistakes will be minimized. The Inuit had no such protected environment and so could not enjoy the luxury of trial and error.

The questions the teacher asks of students are not genuine questions. The teacher already knows the answer to his or her own question, and the students know the teacher knows the answer. So the exercise, the heart of formal learning, is disingenuous, it is a game with complex rules that defy common logic. Commonsense logic would dictate that you ask questions when you need information and do not know the answer, but at school you only ask questions when you already know the answer.

Imagine how bizarre this whole exercise would seem to Inuit students. No wonder they seem unresponsive to mainstream teachers. Indeed, the widespread stereotype that Inuit students are unresponsive is reinforced by my own longitudinal research on the linguistic and cognitive development of Inuit students. Evidence that the "asking questions that you already know the answers to ritual" may explain the unresponsiveness of Inuit students emerged in a most surprising manner. It just so happened that one of our Inuit testers was blind. We were amazed by how verbal the students were when our blind tester asked about different colors or to describe a picture. Clearly, our blind tester could not see the material she was questioning about, and so students felt compelled to offer as much information as they could. Conversely, the exercise no doubt seemed ridiculous when a sighted tester asked questions about colors and pictures.

But this process begins even before children enter kindergarten. Mainstream parents spend an inordinate amount of time asking their children questions, not for information, but as a mechanism to encourage and test learning. Children will be asked to name the colors that the parent points to in turn. Children will be read the same story dozens of times with the parent pausing to ask the child questions about the story, the characters, the setting, and, "What is going to happen next?" Parents will engage in number games with children, and the "in thing" is for parents to watch carefully selected television programs with their children and then question them about the program's content. In all these instances, the parents are asking questions to which they already know the answer.

The children are learning a cultural ritual that lies at the heart of formal learning. It is a complex ritual for it requires the child understanding that, in certain circumstances, one asks questions to obtain information, but in a learning context the child will be asked questions by adults who already know the answer. Nevertheless, to be successful, the child must assume or pretend that the adult does not know the answer. Only by successfully pretending can the child rationalize answering as if providing enlightenment to the adult. I have a suspicion that children will occasionally give a purposefully wrong answer in order to check the adult's reaction. This allows the child to confirm her or his implicit assumption about how the ritual is supposed to unfold. That is, when the child offers a wrong answer, the parent will quickly remind the child of the right answer. This confirms for the child that the ritual does indeed require giving answers that are already known by the parent.

This fundamental ritual is essential to a lifetime of formal learning, it begins early in the child's development, and it is implicit. Children who are not socialized into this implicit culture early will experience difficulty in any formal school environment. Such students will appear to be smart enough to the teacher, but they will always manage to not quite deliver what is required to perform well in a formal classroom. Clearly this puts many students at a disadvantage.

In summary, I believe that in order to understand the pervasive underachievement experienced by colonized people, it is essential to appreciate the identity vacuum they confront. At the basis of identity issues is the relationship between heritage cultures and European culture. I have argued that the relationship can best be characterized by a form of internal colonialism, but one that leaves colonized people with only a fragmented schema of the heritage culture and European culture to draw upon.

Valueless Colonialism and the Self-Concept

My prototype of the psychologically healthy individual is one who possesses a clearly defined collective and personal identity along with a reasonably high collective and personal self-esteem. Armed with this idealized self-concept, any individual is prepared to engage in meaningful and purposive interaction with his or her physical and social environment. As well, he or she is prepared to deal with a changing world.

The immediate challenge is to understand the necessary conditions for the development of a healthy self-concept. Since the focus of the present volume is on group-related social problems, it would seem reasonable to begin with group-based self-definition and self-esteem.

Presumably a clearly defined group-based self-definition or collective identity requires that the individual receive from his or her group a consistent and clearly defined set of elements. If every member of my cultural group expresses the same cultural history, the same core values, the same attitudes, and the same action priorities, then I am certain to develop a clearly defined collective identity.

My analysis of valueless colonialism makes clear the implications for the self-definition component of the self-concept. First, members of colonized groups are required to integrate two very different cultures in some unspecified proportion. Beyond this, as we have seen, neither of the contributing cultural models, mainstream culture or the heritage culture, are themselves clear. The result is that it is virtually impossible for members of colonized groups to develop a clearly defined collective identity.

The consequences of this impossibility are devastating. First, no member of the group will have a clearly defined collective identity. Second, as a result, it will be difficult for any colonized individual to develop a clearly defined personal identity. Personal aspects of self-definition arise from commerce that the individual has with members of his or her own group, which allows the person to gain some perspective on what characteristics make him or her unique, different, or special. How can a personal definition emerge in a context where there is no clearly defined collective identity? It is impossible to be different when there is no sameness against which to measure potential differences.

For precisely the same reasons, collective and personal self-esteem are problematic. Developing self-esteem requires comparing one's self to some standard. What happens when there is no standard, that is, where there is no collective identity upon which to make an evaluation? The individual who suffers from low self-esteem confronts a major challenge, but at least the problem is clear. People may not be accurate when they make their evaluation, perhaps they are better than they think, perhaps they need to commit themselves to improvement so that over time the results of the evaluative process will be more positive. Finally, perhaps the person needs to build his or her self-esteem on other dimensions of his or her self-definition. These problems associated with low self-esteem, potentially destructive as they are, nevertheless are comprehensible and so at least meaningful interventions can be contemplated.

Where there is no standard or clear collective and, by extension, personal identity to even use as a point of comparison, then questions of self-esteem are not just problematic, they are impossible. The current logic evoking low self-esteem as an explanation for academic underachievement and social problems goes something like this. Colonized groups have low status and little power. Their interactions with advantaged mainstream groups and institutions is a constant reminder of their inferiority. This constant nega-tive feedback becomes internalized in the form of pervasive low self-esteem, which translates into the person believing that she or he is inca-pable and incompetent.

My own analysis is far more devastating. Members of colonized groups have no clear image of their heritage culture or of mainstream culture upon which to build a collective identity. With no blueprint for life, it becomes impossible for people to develop any clearly defined personal identity. Moreover, they have no basis for assessing themselves in order to build self-esteem. The final result is not merely an internalized state of incompe-tence but a profound lack of self-identification and comprehension. Colo-nized people are not just down on themselves, they are lost.

CHAPTER 6

Collective Identity Overload: A Threat to Society's Most Disadvantaged and Not So Disadvantaged Groups

For severely disadvantaged groups, the normal challenge of building a clearly defined collective identity is rendered impossible by the need to juggle competing collective identities that are devoid of meaningful content because of an extreme power differential between them. But there is yet another set of social circumstances conspiring against collective identity development: collective identity overload. Simply stated, when an individual is confronted with too many collective identity alternatives, the result is profound confusion.

Collective identity overload is not just a threat to the identity of severely disadvantaged group members but impacts everyone. What I am arguing is that collective identity overload is a pervasive societal problem. In order to appreciate its widespread impact, we need to explore the phenomenon of ethnic nationalism including political separation movements and the plight of mainstream young and not so young people. Having described the effects of collective identity overload for society in general, we can proceed to examine its effects on the already decimated collective identity of severely disadvantaged group members.

ETHNIC NATIONALISM AND POLITICAL SEPARATION

Beginning in the late 1960s and early 1970s, the so-called ethnic revolution began. All over North America, and indeed throughout the world, came new expressions of ethnic pride and solidarity. New labels were introduced, ranging from Black power to Red power (First Nations), and every American and Canadian became hyphenated with ethnic qualifiers. All of a sudden, people emphasized their ethnic affiliation. They were no longer Canadian but Italian-Canadian or Greek-Canadian or every conceivable ethnic identity. So widespread was the movement that mainstream White North Americans felt left out of the process, having no compelling ethnic identity with which to identify. New romantic images emerged. Once America was described as a "melting pot," a huge cauldron where newcomers were thrown in, the heat was turned up, and the contents stirred vigorously. With enough heat and stirring, all traces of the heritage culture would melt away or perhaps evaporate if the pot reached the boiling point. In a complete turnaround, the melting pot image was replaced with an image of society as a "mosaic," "tossed salad," "patchwork quilt," or "rainbow coalition."

The ethnic revolution was not limited to North America. The Soviet Union experienced a similar movement, and I can remember witnessing identical phenomena while living in the Philippines and India. Ethnolinguistic groups in each country were championing their ethnolinguistic identity, and each nation was in the process of trying to reduce the importance of English, a colonial language.

The same epoch produced, the reunification of Germany notwithstanding, a plethora of political separation movements that were rooted in ethnic identity. In North America, the Quebec separation movement is prototypic, but examples include the Basques of Spain and even the Scots and Welsh of Great Britain. The breakup of the former Soviet Union and Yugoslavia are similar prototypic examples.

There are two features of the ethnic revolution that make it an especially interesting phenomenon. First, social scientists in the early 1970s began describing North American society as multicultural and ethnically diverse, thereby challenging the received wisdom that ethnic groups inevitably give up their heritage culture when they come to North America. Of course, writers in the United States were prone to describe multiculturalism as a genuine revolution against the assimilative melting pot, whereas Canadian social scientists depicted Canada as a mosaic that always promoted multiculturalism, so the revolution was more a revitalization than a revolution.

You would think that forward-thinking social scientists had spearheaded the ethnic movement, but such was not the case. In fact, it was a genuine populist movement initiated by citizens of every ethnic persuasion, and only after a rise in ethnic vitality did social scientists begin writing about the phenomenon.

Second, the ethnic revolution was a complete surprise. It flew in the rational face of all that was happening in global communication. The world was becoming a global village, where every corner of the world was instantly accessible to everyone. It was felt that the world was becoming more cosmopolitan and that soon every individual would feel like a citizen of the world, geographic boundaries would disappear, and local ethnic identities would become obsolete. Have not multinational corporations spearheaded the new reality?

So why in the face of global communication did the ethnic revolution begin? While everyone marveled at how global communication would bring people together, no one considered its psychological ramifications. People were now bombarded with so many different social realities, so many different lifestyles, so many different values, beliefs, and attitudes that their collective identity was threatened. Global communication generated a need in people to reaffirm their collective identity. Specifically, the need was for defining a local or very circumscribed collective identity and also one that touched on all of life's important domains. The perfect candidate for such a collective identity would be one's cultural identity. And, thus, the rise of ethnic nationalism and the desire for political separation represented a psychological response to the threats to collective identity posed by the collective identity overload of global communication.

At a superficial level, this is a phenomenon we have all experienced. One immediate response to traveling in a different culture, aside from the excitement and enjoyment of the experience, is the reaffirmation of one's own cultural identity. Travelers upon their return home are often heard to proclaim, "I never realized how much I appreciate my own country!" At a more profound level, reaffirming one's primary cultural identity provides the individual with a solid collective identity base that can serve as protection in the face of global exposure to competing social realities. Cultural identity serves as a bulwark against collective identity overload.

Young Mainstream North Americans

A revitalized cultural identity as a constructive response to social identity overload can be effective if, and only if, the individual has a clearly defined cultural identity to rely on. Young people today are often described as the lost generation. According to pop analysis, they are lost because they have no moral, social, or economic compass. In short, they have no clearly defined collective identity.

Even I, as a baby boomer, can appreciate that information overload can challenge the structure of one's collective identity. Perhaps some simple examples from less than crucial domains of daily life can illustrate the point. I used to know that exercise was good for me, and so, fortunately, ice hockey and bicycling are part of my lifestyle and not only bring me pleasure, but also make me feel self-righteous about the fact that exercise is actually good for me. With today's information overload, I confront a trivial "identity" crisis. I am told that hockey is bad for my heart because it requires quick bursts of energy followed by two minutes of rest, and my knees apparently are not built to take the torque required by the sport (any hockey player knows that, we just do not want to be told). Bicycling is going to ruin my back, and I am going to get head injuries and lose too much salt, and on and on.

Needless to say, lacing on a pair of skates or cycling on an abandoned road have become traumatic experiences, to say nothing of my eating habits. Again, once it was all so simple. You were supposed to eat in moderation from all food groups, and the better it tasted the worse it was for you. Because I was never very good with the moderation bit, I would follow these simple rules and skip meals when weight became a problem, which was and is most of the time. Again, with the information explosion, all semblance of eating guidelines are lost. The list of what is bad for me has reached such proportions that by the time I analyze whether I am eating good or bad cholesterol or whether my lettuce has been doused with pesticides, I am afraid to eat anything but a sugar doughnut. The point of these two trivial examples is that any semblance of self-definition that might serve as my guide in these simple domains is obliterated in the face of information overload. These examples are frustrating little challenges to my identity, and I can easily retreat into a collective and personal identity, carved out over many years, to cope with the overload. But these small examples can become catastrophic when applied to challenges in the area of fundamental values, ideologies, and lifestyles, and where there is no well-defined identity to serve as a buffer.

Identity overload has consequences that serve to alienate us not only from each other, but also from any coherent purpose. Again, I can only draw on my own personal experience in order to capture the everyday way in which I become alienated from any shared lens on reality.

I begin with my academic work environment where I, like everyone else, am overwhelmed by the sheer volume of published research that has accelerated knowledge to the point that I simply cannot keep up. But this scientific information overload has a number of consequences beyond my scramble to keep up and my becoming more selective in what new information I attend to. This information explosion alienates me from my colleagues.

Work-related conversations with my colleagues used to be easy and informative. I could walk into any office and ask, "So what did you think of that bizarre set of findings reported by whoever" and be guaranteed a response ranging from indifference to an emotional harangue. The point is, I would get some reaction because, and only because, I could be virtually certain that all of my colleagues were reading the same journals. Today, no two of my colleagues are familiar with the same journals, theories, names, or controversies. Specialties within disciplines have become increasingly narrow because of the explosion in information. Because of information overload, there is no mechanism for shared academic interests to serve as a facilitator of social interaction. But more important, the lack of academic connection means that I have lost informal ways to test my perceptions and intellectual analyses of new ideas. And, as an academic, that loss is more important than the practical issue of keeping up with the avalanche of new information.

I grew up in a context where everyone played sports. Okay, it is true that sports were organized mostly for boys, and there were some boys who did not play sports. But the number of sports was very limited. Being a Canadian, we all played ice hockey, and some of us played football. Oh yes, there were other sports, like tennis and swimming and skiing, but you played hockey and, in addition, did these other sports. At that time, there were very few professional teams of any consequence, so even if you did not play the sport, everyone followed the professional teams and sports offered up a ready-made shared basis for much discussion; everyone knew enough about the default sports to participate in discussions: boys, girls, young, and old.

Today, there is a vast array of sports and exercise opportunities. There is an endless variety of professional sports teams involving everything from beach volleyball and ultimate Frisbee to luge and box lacrosse. Rationally, I applaud these developments because they allow more people to participate either actively or as spectators. But emotionally, something is missing. What is missing is being able to talk about sports with everyone from the cab driver to colleagues to family. No two are engaged in the same sport, and so there is no shared basis for connecting.

The theme repeats itself with respect to the proliferation of specialty channels on television. The offerings are so vast that no two people watch the same programs. You can't approach anyone you meet and say, "So who do you think shot JR?" And the point goes way beyond the opportunity for casual conversation around the water cooler. Informal conversations about television programs and, by extension, films, the hottest music, and the latest bestseller were opportunities to share values, check perceptions, and contemplate one's moral compass. In a relatively recent movie, a man offers a couple a million dollars for the opportunity to make love to the other man's wife. Imagine the discussions such a premise would generate among a group of men and women who had seen the film? Talk about a challenge to collective and personal identity.

The positive consequences to the explosion in information and participatory opportunities are readily apparent. But they also serve to alienate in the sense that there are fewer and fewer people being exposed to, or engaging in, the same events. This has to have an impact on the number of shared connections among members of the same group and, by extension, it has to make it more difficult for a group's collective identity to retain its shared clarity in terms of goals and values.

As I proofread this chapter, it is one week to the day since the savage terrorist attack on the World Trade Center in New York and the Pentagon in Washington, D.C. There are, of course, multiple dimensions and layers to this tragic event, but one that underscores my point here is the truly collective response to the disaster.

In times of disaster, we are reminded of how they "bring people together." Political rivals unite, geographical and competing political agendas are put aside, and, indeed, ordinary citizens of every conceivable walk of life embrace one another. One feature of this process is the extent to which the magnitude of the disaster ensures that it is a preoccupation for everyone. For example, in the past week, I scanned every one of over 200 channels, and every single channel carried a 24-hour coverage of the terrorist attack. It is the only time in recent history that everyone was glued to the same theme. It represents a rare time when literally everyone is focused on the same precise event. The result is that there is a shared basis for interaction among any two random persons throughout the nation. Normally, on an everyday basis, two citizens drawn at random would share very little in terms of experience. The attacks on the World Trade Center and the Pentagon are a horrible exception. But they point to the need for shared experiences upon which to build a collective identity. With some orchestration, perhaps collective identities could be strengthened without having to count on unanticipated disasters, human or otherwise.

Identity Overload

No doubt the most articulate exposé of the psychological consequences of information overload is Kenneth Gergen's (1991) appropriately titled book, *The Saturated Self: Dilemmas of Identity in Contemporary Life*. Gergen lists the 20th-century technologies that have rendered our lives seemingly unmanageable. The list includes the classic technologies that rapidly expanded during this century, such as rail, mail, car, phone, radio, movies, and print publishing. To this list, he adds the more recent and revolutionary technologies of air travel, TV, and electronic communication through computer technology. All these conspire to immerse us in many more relationships, which requires such frenetic energy that no one of them seems satisfying and all seem shallow and fleeting.

For Gergen, this is the essential feature of postmodernism, which he contrasts with romanticism and modernism. The romantic period, he notes, was characterized by the self being defined in terms of deeply felt inner states such as passion, eternal love, inspiration, grief, creativity, and genius. These are what gave life its meaning and were the basis for building identity. With the emergence of modernism, objective reason and observation became the cornerstone of meaning. That is, the self could be known through commerce with what is observable and, naturally, the less grounded concepts of romanticism were rejected.

The modernist was grounded in the observable and pursued well-defined, self-centered goals. All this is not possible for the postmodernist, who has so many selves as to reach saturation. Gergen recognizes that the overloaded self is an uncomfortable state and is sensitive to the widespread societal belief that something fundamental has been lost. Where Gergen is especially challenging is in his refusal to conclude that the postmodern self is essentially destructive. His argument is that, while the self may need to be redefined, that aim is not only possible but ultimately, perhaps, genuinely constructive. The adjustment will be constructive in the sense that old-fashioned self-centeredness will need to give way to new identities rooted in social relationships, with the outcome being a greater sense of relatedness and belonging.

Gergen may be right, but what happens while these adjustments to postmodernism are being made? The answer is a people who are lost. And young people are especially vulnerable. We older types likely cling to a form of modernism that, in today's world, is no longer completely functional. But at least it provides us with a clear collective identity, one that allows us to complain about changes and lament the past when life seemed understandable. We can poke fun at automatic voice messaging and bank machines while struggling with job uncertainty and the pressures of e-mail and fax, which speed up our lives. And when the pressure becomes too much and our sense of self is threatened, we can look to each other and reminisce about the past: a past when a relationship meant something, a company respected its employees, and, on the phone or at the bank, you could talk to a real person.

Young people are not so fortunate. What do they have to return to? Even if Gergen is right, we need to recognize that an incoherent collective identity, fueled by information overload, is the issue and we need to focus on speeding up the process of articulating this new postmodern identity.

Gergen's analysis is also highly abstract. As such, it is challenging in its conceptual distinctions between romanticism, modernism, and postmodernism. But what does this mean for the everyday identities of people attempting to navigate postmodernism? In times past, the everyday person understood himself or herself and pursued meaningful life goals against the backdrop of a collective identity. That collective identity spelled out not only what to pursue and why to pursue it but also the details of how to pursue it and, in the process, how to evaluate progress on the journey.

Young people, generally, and young men, in particular, face information overload with respect to the most important spheres of their lives, areas where a clear collective identity is essential to providing guidance and meaning. I emphasize young men because I will argue that, while young women also face identity overload, they do have one very important component of identity that has become an identity mission: to take their rightful place in all those societal domains where they have previously been denied full participation.

Young people today have been denied a clearly defined collective identity, even with respect to the most fundamental domains. Any North American collective identity will include a belief in basic societal institutions including democracy, justice, policing, education, religion, and human relationships. Not too long ago, people understood what these institutions were and believed they lived up to their stated standards of conduct. None was ever perfect and so people would react with outrage when they received information that violated their basic identity. When a crooked judge was exposed, a politician lied, or a teacher abused his or her power, outrage followed because people believed in the integrity of the collective identity and felt that even one violation might chip away at that precious identity.

What are young people today facing? Insight into their lost identity came for me when I was coaching a football team of 17- and 18-year-old men. I would hear them rave about the videos they watched, all of which featured excessive violence and some larger-than-life character like Rambo. In a fit of needing to "get with it," I rented several of their favorites and, as you might imagine, spent one of the longest weekends of my life.

At first, every movie seemed to be the same endless violence punctuated by a car chase or a chase involving some high-speed machinery. Only toward the end of my vigil did it dawn on me that there was a similar theme to all the movies: The enemy in each case was not the usual array of standard outgroup members but society's own institutions. The enemy was us and took the form of a corrupt military establishment, small-town police force, justice system, or political machine. In the past, the custom for every action film was to create monsters out of, and dehumanize, outgroup members. The outgroups ranged from countries that waged war against democracy, Aboriginal people and Mexicans who had the audacity to protect their lands, and crooks and "bad guys" who were clearly in violation of our collective identity. Choosing these targets did little to reduce our ethnocentrism, but in an indirect way they served to reinforce our collective identity. Young people are deluged with enemies that represent the legacy from which their own collective identity would spring. How can a collective identity survive the onslaught so that internal enemies are no more the exception but the rule.

More generally, what has happened to the North American dream, that shared template of how life should unfold? Everybody used to know the formula. First, you go to school, play sports, and learn to play a musical instrument. Next, you choose a university or technical stream at high school and develop not too serious relationships with the opposite sex; you might "go steady" but that would worry mom and dad. Then life gets serious: you pursue your career or vocation, marry the person of your dreams for life, have 2.2 children and a dog, and, ultimately, have your own home. It all sounds so simple, indeed somewhat boring upon reflection. Much fun is made of this collective identity. Those who are pursuing the formula the closest can be heard to say, "There is no way I'm going to end up with a tacky house in the suburbs with two kids and a skinny tree on the lawn." But such mockery is the clearest indication of just how ingrained our collective identity was.

For young people today, no such collective identity exists. The prototypic lifelong marriage and family structure has been fragmented to the point that young people are subjected to such an overload in terms of possible models that crafting a collective identity is impossible. Schooling, which occupies so many hours and years of a young person's life, has become irrelevant. In my day, we used to wonder why school was important and question the pragmatic value of Latin and mathematics. But our parents, extended family, teachers, community leaders, and societal heroes all emphasized its importance. We may not have been totally convinced, but deep down we were aware that somehow education and training were important. Not today. The old idea of career advancement being built upon certain clearly defined educational and training requirements and hard work has become a maze of confusion. In the old days, the big decision was whether to take Latin or science. Today, under the guise of providing young people with more opportunities, schools offer unlimited options; students do not fail, they simply glide into some new "special" program, prerequisites to advance from one level to the next are nonexistent, and there are so many educational and training institutions, certificates, papers, degrees, and specializations that no sane young person can internalize any clear definition for their education.

The world of work is equally confusing. People work part-time, flex hours, and out of their home, and the global economy offers no clear guidelines for how to "get ahead" or "make it" economically. Moreover, government assistance programs offer such an array of specialized offerings that no one can assimilate the information.

In times of a clearly defined collective identity, the consequences of identity overload stand out as a feared aberration. Consider the fretful parents from a small town whose son or daughter has just headed off to a university to live in residence, or worse an apartment, for the first time. What is their overriding concern? They are petrified that their dutiful sons and daughters are going to become corrupted by university life. Never mind the avant-garde ideas they may be exposed to in their classes, it is the social life that has parents worried.

What are the social dynamics at the root of parents' concerns? Until the fateful day that they reach university age, their son or daughter has been brought up in a home, school, church, recreational context, and community that espouses a consistent set of values, morals, ideology, and attitudes. Young people have no choice but to develop a clearly defined collective identity that is entirely comprehensible and supported by parents and anyone else in authority for that matter. The fear is that at the university, the young person will be exposed to a wide variety of competing social realities, that most of these competing social realities are socially destructive, and that the young person will redefine his or her collective identity in terms of one of these negative social realities.

Our fretful parents will be anxiously awaiting Thanksgiving, Christmas, and Easter visits from their children, antennas alert for any signs that their children have been influenced by party-going radicals. But even if parents' worst fears are realized, at least the problem is clear. The dutiful son or daughter has strayed from his or her values by internalizing a new collective identity, and serious intervention is required.

But there is a potentially worse fate. Some students are confronted with so many different social realities at a university that they are overwhelmed by the array of choices confronting them. The result may be that their self-definition crumbles, leaving them with absolutely no idea of who they are or where they are going. The consequences are that, instead of scaring their parents with a new collective and personal identity, they become totally lost. What parents will see is their son or daughter completely devoid of goals, ambition, passion, caring, or involvement with life. Like colonized peoples who have no clearly defined social reality around which to build a self-definition, our university student is exposed to such a wide variety of social realities that he or she is completely immobilized.

It is this proliferation of competing social realities that is confronting all young people, not just elite university students. Traditional authorities and institutions that used to provide symbolic role models for self-definition have fallen into disrepute. More important, everywhere they look, no clear social reality emerges. Mainstream society offers so many different models for what constitutes a family that integrating a clearly defined self-definition as a guide is lost. There are so many competing definitions of "man" and "woman" that gender definition is confusing.

My analysis has focused on young people generally, but I believe it is young men who are especially vulnerable in terms of their collective identity. Young women are exposed to the same dizzying array of identity templates as young men, and, of course, one of the sources of confusion is the rapidly changing role of women brought on by the women's movement. It is intriguing to me that the pop phrase of the day is the "changing role of women." I know that it was women who had the courage to instigate change in order to redress a legacy of social injustice, but the concept of "role" is not an individual concept but a relational one. For every role there is a counterrole: parent-child, boss-employee, leader-follower and, yes, man-woman. Thus, any change to the role of "woman" will have its reciprocal effect on the role of "man." Therefore, I much prefer the phrase "changing gender roles."

The changes in the reciprocal gender roles have created collective identity confusion. Before these changes, when collective identity was clear, interacting with members of the opposite sex was simple. Men worked, earned the money, made the big decisions in the home, initiated courtships, suffered stress-related diseases, and had all the status. Women flirted with education to pursue a man, stayed at home to raise a family, the kitchen became the woman's fiefdom and they passively accepted a man's romantic advances and had little status in society. As unfair as it was, it was a clearly defined collective identity.

As women instigated a change in status for their role, and by implication the role of men, the formerly clear collective identity became useless. The result was, and is, uncertainty and anxiety about what behavior is appropriate. Men agonize over whether the woman they are with is "traditional" or "liberated," each identity requiring a very different set of behaviors. Bizarre social scenarios are being acted out in boardrooms across North America. Picture the monthly sales meeting chaired by the male boss and his 10-person sales staff, all of whom are men, except for Donna. The old collective identity was so easy. Mr. Boss would arrive at the meeting two minutes after the appointed hour to find his sales staff in place and eagerly waiting. The first order of business would be for Mr. Boss to indicate to Donna that 11 cups of coffee were required with assorted configurations of sugar, artificial sweetener, cream, and sugar. But with gender roles in flux, and no clear collective identity, Mr. Boss arrives at the meeting and immediately faces a dilemma. He cannot ask Donna to chase up the coffee, for that would violate some new gender rules. He knows that if he asks any one of his male employees, they will, because of vestiges of the old collective identity, be insulted at being given such a demeaning request. (Does it dawn on Mr. Boss that if it is demeaning for his male employees, for years it must have been equally demeaning for women?) And so Mr. Boss is trapped, and only one solution presents itself—he will get the coffee himself. And as he returns from his quest performing a circus juggling act and feeling that he will endear himself to his sales staff, he is struck by a thought. What will I do for the next meeting?

My theory of the self was critical of the overemphasis on having a positive self and joined other self-theorists who emphasize the need for a well-defined and consistent self. Having meaning to one's life is, I believe, more important than artificially feeling good about oneself. Indeed, I have theorized that one cannot engage the evaluative process unless the self has been clearly defined.

We expect young people to self-regulate, to eschew immediate gratification for long-term benefit. To ask young people to forgo immediate satisfaction requires a collective identity that is clear and a consensus that is unanimous. Identity overload offers so many options that responding to immediate gratification is as viable an option as any other. Indeed, our young people confront a culture that promotes buy now pay later, buy a lottery ticket for the quick fix, medicate yourself for every ailment, focus on your rights not your duties, trust no one, and do not even begin to put order into the array of mothers, fathers, step-mothers and step-fathers, siblings and step-siblings, and extended families and step-families that confuse you at every turn. This nightmare becomes obvious when my students go home for the holidays and wrestle with whom they will visit and when and why. Most would prefer to stay in town and "hang" with their friends.

Street kids represent the ultimate retreat from these complexities. They have reduced life to its simplest: survival on the streets. To survive takes skill, not just in the sense of being tough but in capitalizing on the myriad agencies and bureaucracies that serve the young. And their logic is unassailable: Being high on drugs feels better than not being high when there is no long-term goal to be compromised, and prostitution is indeed the quickest way to earn money, again when there is no long-term goal to be compromised.

Identity Overload and the Disadvantaged

If mainstream members of cultural groups and young people are psychologically challenged to cope with identity overload, what impact does it have on members of society's most disadvantaged groups? The impact is devastating, and nowhere is this more dramatically illustrated than the case of the Inuit of the high Arctic.

Technological advances are difficult enough to keep up with and to psychologically integrate for mainstream North Americans. Imagine its impact on, for example, the Inuit who are introduced to the accumulation of technology overnight. I remember as a boy jumping for joy when my dad would let me visit my friend's house down the street to watch television. They were one of the few to have a television; there was only one channel, but I loved "Hockey Night in Canada," "The Honeymooners," and "Ed Sullivan." Eventually we got our own set; two channels were functional, and we focused on how to receive some of the American stations. Attention then shifted to color TV, and then cable became standard. Today, I am contemplating how to cope with hundreds of channels—talk about information overload.

The point here is that the slow accommodation to developments in television allowed me to integrate the technology into my life. But even this slow evolution accommodation was not very successful. Witness the growing debate among parents about how to limit and monitor their children's viewing habits.

Imagine the adjustment required for the Inuit of the high Arctic who have television introduced to them all at once, in color, with a multitude of channels, coming from bizarre places like Edmonton, Atlanta, and Detroit. The nightly news from Detroit is like outer space for someone living in a remote village of 400 people, to say nothing of making sense of "As the World Turns" and "World Federation Wrestling."

An equally striking example can be found at the grocery store. Mainstream visitors to Arctic communities or First Nation reserves are shocked to find everyone living on a diet of potato chips, cookies, bubble gum, and Coke. You cannot even buy diet Coke. "Beyond Yuppie" mainstreamers forget the history of their own eating habits. They grew up with the slow introduction of junk food and fast-food restaurants. With the introduction of each new tacky foodstuff, they gorged themselves until they and their parents brought a little moderation to the process. And with the development of artificial sweeteners, people like me can still overdose on caffeine and overindulge, firm in the belief that we are following a healthy lifestyle.

When Aboriginal communities are instantly deluged with an overwhelming array of foods that taste different yet good, and are trendy, is it any wonder that there is for the moment no clearly defined game plan to curtail excesses?

But let us turn our attention to formal schooling. Formal schooling occupies a good portion of young peoples' time and preoccupation. Moreover, formal schooling for mainstreamers is intimately associated with intellectual, occupational, social, and moral development. Thus, it is a key component for collective identity.

Mainstreamers know firsthand the experience of formal schooling, as did their parents, grandparents, and great-grandparents. Thus, parents socialize their children with a clearly defined template about formal schooling. But even mainstream parents are struggling with the accelerated changes in school philosophy, constantly changing curricula, and the social and moral disruptions in school missions.

For society's most disadvantaged groups, formal schooling is completely bewildering. With no history of formal schooling themselves, parents have difficulty communicating a coherent set of identity guidelines to their children.

Mainstream parents may gain some superficial insight into this bewilderment by contemplating the introduction of computers to the school and the home. Schools, mainly because adult teachers themselves feel lost with computers, have no idea how to integrate computers into the curriculum. Parents feel virtually lost, hesitant to even touch a computer, while their children bang on the keyboard with reckless abandon. When parents tentatively move the mouse, they somehow manage to move the cursor off the screen, while their children whip the cursor around with the mouse clicking a mile a minute.

But at a more fundamental level, the mere dislocation of gender roles, representing only one component of a collective identity, has profound implications. Beyond the amusing confusion lie the enormous adjustment problems. Where are the role models of both men and women in terms of how to juggle work and family roles? Must the world of commerce and politics be completely redefined in terms of changing gender roles? There simply is no template or collective identity to provide the answer. Multiply the gender identity issue to every life domain and our young people are like a deer paralyzed in the headlights of an oncoming car.

In summary, severely disadvantaged groups have had change thrust on them so rapidly that they confront identity overload that ultimately leads to confusion in terms of collective identity. Ironically, the explosion in information technology and basic role changes have meant that mainstreamers are beginning to suffer the consequences of information overload. Mainstreamers are not overloaded nearly as much as those who are severely disadvantaged, but the consequences are beginning to surface in the form of confusion in collective identity.

CHAPTER 7

Collective Demotivation

Motivation is the psychological engine that propels human behavior. It is what energizes behavior in a particular direction. Much of society's attention is taken up with those who are energized in the wrong direction. Sexual predators, drug dealers, criminals, and terrorists all display motivation: What is wrong with their energy is the direction that their energy takes. I will argue that, in the case of society's most disadvantaged groups, value-less colonialism and identity overload have conspired to produce an even more frightening problem. The problem is not misdirected motivation but the complete lack of the energy and direction associated with motivation: in short, demotivation.

In order to illustrate the argument, I will focus on the domain of education, but the processes and consequences apply to all of life's key domains. Put another way, because cultural identity cuts across all life domains, its motivational consequences will be felt everywhere, and what applies to formal education can be taken as prototypic for any aspect of life that is touched by cultural identity.

When a teacher describes a student as lacking in motivation, we quickly picture a student who does not attend school regularly, does not work hard, rarely does homework, does not listen in class, and appears not to care about the consequences. The same student may even be disruptive in class, leading the teacher to become anxious about class discipline. Our challenge here is to understand what motivation is so that we can create learning environments that maximize the chances for students to be motivated toward constructive ends.

Motivation is absolutely fundamental to human behavior because it is the process that gives direction and purpose to a person's behavior. The motivated student is one who directs his or her behavior toward achieving in school and who pursues that goal with energy and a sense of purpose. In short, motivation is the cause, while accomplishment is the effect. Motivation, of course, can be applied to any human domain, and so a person might be motivated to maintain good interpersonal relationships or to become an excellent hockey player. Whatever the domain, motivation is a characteristic of the person that points his or her energy and behavior in a particular direction.

We begin our analysis of motivation by noting, first, that motivation is a property of a person, not the environment. While teachers might try to create an environment that facilitates or encourages motivation, ultimately the motivation must become a central component of the student's psychological makeup. Second, motivation is forward-looking and futuristic, not rooted in the present or past. That is, motivation points to the future in the sense that it involves a person directing his or her energy toward some future goal.

One of the most comprehensive reviews of human motivation has been provided by Ford (1992), and his theoretical model, motivational systems theory, can serve as a useful framework for outlining the rudiments of motivation. Ford views motivation as "the organized patterning of three psychological functions that serve to direct, energize, and regulate goal-directed activity: personal goals, emotional arousal processes, and personal agency beliefs."

Ford's model can be described in terms of the following formula:

MOTIVATION = GOALS x EMOTIONS x AGENCY BELIEFS

This formula can serve as a useful guide to our discussion of the three key psychological functions.

PERSONAL GOALS

Personal goals are individuals' thoughts about the desired states or outcomes they would like to achieve or ones they would like to avoid. A person's goal may be as simple and short-term as finishing a mathematics problem before lunch or as long-term and abstract as obtaining a university degree. Moreover, personal goals can refer to every domain of life, including those that involve work or school; human relationships; personal, physical, and psychological health; and leisure activities and hobbies.

Personal goals are, clearly, essential for motivation. A person with no goal has no blueprint for action. Only a goal can serve to channel a person's behavior in a particular direction. The student whose goal is to successfully master course material can use that goal to direct behavior, just as the student whose goal is to disrupt the class will have his or her behavior focused in a different direction. But both students do have a goal, and, thus, each has a blueprint for action, the difference lies in the direction of their behavior. However, for the student who has no goal, there can only be demotivation, that is, aimless behavior or little or no behavior at all.

The aim, therefore, is to help the individual articulate a goal and, hopefully, to articulate one that is personally and socially constructive. Goals that are most motivating have certain characteristics. First, the goal must be *clear*. If the goal is vague, it is difficult for the person to chart the best course of action in order to achieve the goal.

Second, goals must be set at the appropriate *level*. If the only goal is one that is far into the future and large in its scope, then it is difficult for the person to be motivated on a day-to-day basis. Similarly, having only a small short-term goal may not be motivating because the individual has trouble envisaging where the achievement of the short-term goal is leading. The most motivating circumstances arise when goals are multileveled and linked to one another. For example, the young student might have the long-term goal of becoming an airline pilot. Becoming a pilot first requires setting the goal of completing high school; even more specifically it requires selecting the right configuration of high school courses and, then, passing them successfully. Finally, the ultimate goal of becoming a pilot requires that the student pass his or her mathematics exam this afternoon. In this example, the student has goals at a variety of levels, and the short-term goals reinforce the medium-range goals that, in turn, reinforce the ultimate goal of becoming a pilot.

Third, motivation is enhanced when the same behavior serves *multiple goals*. Suppose, for example, that when our student pursues the goal of becoming a pilot, he or she is simultaneously able to achieve additional goals such as gaining respect from family and friends, earning an excellent salary, and being able to travel. Anytime the same behavior can serve a variety of goals, the motivation to achieve any one of the goals will be stronger.

Finally, goals should be *optimally challenging*. Goals that are too easy to achieve leave the person bored, unfocused, and demotivated. At the other extreme, goals that are virtually impossible to achieve leave the person frustrated and dispirited with the result being a state of demotivation. Part

of the socialization process is helping people take their initial goals and re-
fine them so that they are optimally challenging.

In summary, the first necessary requirement for motivation is having a
goal that can serve to focus and direct the person's behavior. Motivation is
maximized where the goals are clear, where they are multileveled and
linked, where they operate simultaneously, and where they are optimally
challenging.

Emotions

Emotions are fundamental to the purposive and directed behavior associated with motivation. Moreover, the relationship between emotions and
personal goals is mutually reinforcing. When people pursue a personal
goal, they are engaged in activity that they define as important for themselves and therefore are likely to feel positive emotions, such as pleasure
and excitement. These positive emotions, in turn, become associated with
pursuing the goal, and this serves to reinforce the importance of that goal.

If the pursuit of a personal goal itself provokes positive emotions, experiencing some success in achieving the goal will provoke even more positive emotions, such as joy and elation. Of course, when people are thwarted
or unsuccessful in their pursuit of personal goals, negative emotions will be
provoked, such as anger, frustration or discouragement. But, to the extent
that personal goal are maintained, both successes and failures will provoke
emotions or feelings of some kind. It is only when people have no goals and
are, therefore, not motivated that they experience no emotions. There is
only one experience that is worse than the feelings associated with failing
to achieve a goals and that is having no goals and being emotionally unin-
volved with life. Nothing is more frightening to teachers than being confronted with students who apparently do not care about anything.

There is an important relationship involving mutual reinforcement between goals and emotions that needs to be delineated so that we can better
understand how motivation functions. We noted that motivation is a property of the person, and, thus, goals and emotions reside within the person.
It is often difficult for people to consciously specify what their goals are.
Emotions help people with goal definition because they will naturally associate their pleasant feelings with whatever behavior they have just been
performing. The student who feels elated at solving a mathematics problem must conclude, "Gee, I really like math and want to do well at it." Conversely, having a well-defined goal triggers emotions in people when they
experience success or failure in pursuit of that goal.

Because of this relationship between goals and emotions, it is possible for other people in the social environment to help shape the individual's motivation. For example, when a teacher responds emotionally to a student's performance (for example, happiness), the teacher is helping the student formulate a goal. This is because the teacher's emotion is likely to stimulate a similar emotion in the student, and the student's emotion will then be linked to the personal goal that he or she was pursuing.

Moreover, respected people in the social environment can impact on the individual's motivation not only by their emotional reaction but through the feedback they provide. For example, a teacher may make a negative assessment of a student's work (for example, "You can do better than that"). The student may well feel embarrassment or shame, not so much because of the poor work he or she has done, but because of the negative social feedback. The student's feelings thereby impact on two goals: maintaining good relations with teachers and successfully executing academic tasks.

The role of others in affecting a person's motivation, however, needs to be qualified. When a teacher rewards a student for academic achievement, a double message is communicated. On the one hand, the message helps the student define his or her goals. On the other hand, the student may associate academic work with social approval such that the goal of social approval becomes more prominent while the goal of academic achievement itself diminishes. After all, the aim is to have the student feel positive emotions about mastering academic material simply because he or she has mastered the material, not because of the social rewards it generates. Too much social reward may lead the student to pursue academic work only when social approval is ensured, and to be uninterested in academic goals when the teacher is not present.

Finally, the link between goals and emotions draws attention to the importance of encouraging people to develop short-term goals in addition to long-term ones. It is difficult for a student to feel any strong emotion when he or she has accomplished a task that is related to a goal that is years in the future. What is needed to sustain motivation are the strong and immediate emotions that arise when an actual goal has been achieved. Hence, it is important to establish short-term goals but, of course, ones that are linked to more distant goals.

Personal Agency Beliefs

The third component of motivation involves an important set of beliefs that, like goals and emotions, reside within the individual. It is not enough for individuals to have a clear goal, they must believe they have the *capability* and the *opportunity* to achieve the goal. The first belief is one that has received a good deal of attention by psychologists who refer to it as self-efficacy (Bandura, 1977; 1986) or perceived competence (Deci & Ryan, 1985). Essentially, people will not be motivated to pursue a goal unless they believe they are capable of achieving it. The issue is not whether the person can *actually* achieve the goal but rather the extent to which they *believe* they can achieve it. When teachers describe students as having low self-esteem, often they are referring to their observation that the students are not motivated to work because they do not believe they are capable of succeeding.

A motivated person not only believes that he or she is capable of achieving a goal, but also believes that the social context offers him or her the opportunity to achieve the goal. Motivated students must believe, for example, that the school, family, and the community can support their desire to learn and that the successful completion of an academic hurdle will prepare them for further study or a good job.

Our analysis of human motivation has been necessarily superficial, especially given the legacy of theory and research that has illuminated the complexities involved in the process. The underachievement of society's most disadvantaged students is both widespread and profound, and this leads me to conclude that the motivational issues are not subtle. Thus, my analysis focuses on the basics of human motivation.

How Valueless Colonialism and Identity Overload Lead to Collective Demotivation

When an individual student is lacking in motivation, educators focus on the personal characteristics of the student, and his or her family situation, in order to diagnose the problem. But in the case of society's most disadvantaged groups, the lack of motivation is widespread. Therefore, any explanation for this collective diagnosis must lie at the group or intergroup level. I have characterized the intergroup reality as one of "valueless colonialism," and "identity overload" and my aim here is to show how these processes impact on the motivation of severely disadvantaged students. How, then, do valueless colonialism and identity overload affect the three key components of motivation? I believe that only by understanding the roots of collective demotivation can meaningful and constructive change be implemented.

Collective Identity and Personal Goals

I have portrayed colonial relations as forcing colonized groups to confront the task of integrating two very different value systems. This task would be challenging enough, but I have argued, further, that colonialism has disrupted the fundamental values of heritage cultures, on the one hand, and only displayed as an alternative a mainstream culture whose fundamental values have been systematically obscured.

Motivation requires first that a person have a clearly defined goal. For members of colonized groups, arriving at a clearly defined goal requires integrating two competing cultures, a daunting task in and of itself. However, the task is made much more difficult because neither of the competing cultures has been clearly defined. Thus, the very basic requirement for motivated behavior, which is taken for granted by those raised exclusively in the context of a single value system, becomes an inordinate challenge for severely disadvantaged groups, with demotivation being the final outcome.

The kaleidoscope of identity models that surround both disadvantaged peoples and mainstream young people only exacerbates the problem of having clearly defined goals. In the face of so many competing possibilities, the individual is reduced to bewilderment. If mainstream culture is that confusing for mainstream young people, imagine the predicament of individuals from colonized groups who have never been exposed to the essentials of mainstream culture.

Matters are made more difficult when we consider the optimum structure of goals for motivation. That is, having goals that are not only clear, but multileveled and linked, is even more difficult in the context of valueless colonialism. As we noted, while the superficial trappings of European culture were offered to Aboriginal people, the longer term and more fundamental values were never explained or modeled. In the context of education, this meant building schools and forcing students to attend according to a schedule, but never was it explained why formal education was important, how it was linked to a particular economic and social structure, or how learning was programmatic. Without understanding these fundamental underpinnings, and with no experience of formal education themselves, Aboriginal parents were not in a position to formulate any clearly defined set of integrated goals.

Collective Identity and Emotion

We noted that motivation requires that, once a goal has been established, behavior directed at achieving the goal must provoke an emotional response in the person so that he or she will pursue the goal with a sense of purpose. The linking of emotions to constructive goals requires a supporting social environment. That is, the student needs to have teachers, administrators, parents, and extended family members all responding in the same emotional fashion to the student's academic behavior. But when the heritage culture has been ruptured through colonialism, and no clear European template has been provided, people are not clear about what emotional response to make to any particular behavior. The student, therefore, has difficulty becoming enthusiastic about any specific activity and, thus, no coherent behavior patterns are established.

We also noted how motivation is enhanced when behavior meets the objectives of several goals simultaneously. The mainstream student who performs well at school is not only meeting the objectives of well-defined academic goals but is simultaneously meeting goals associated with reinforcing positive relations with teachers, parents, older siblings, and friends. The Aboriginal student may provoke a positive reaction from mainstream teachers, but the achievement may not be reinforced by significant others in the student's social environment.

Finally, the mainstream value of individual-based merit has not been applied to formal education in a manner that is explicit enough for Aboriginal students and parents to formulate clearly defined long- and short-term goals. Violations of the value of meritocracy are not extremely damaging in mainstream society because the violations are offset by an entire cultural ethos that maintains the meritocracy value. Aboriginal people have not been exposed to a clear schema of how a meritocracy functions, and, thus, violations produce only vagueness and confusion, conditions that are not conducive to the formulation of goals. Examples of violations to the meritocracy in Aboriginal communities I have visited include the following partial list, a list that includes items that many mainstream parents are beginning to worry about for their children.

- Aboriginal students are given good grades when they have not met the objectives.

- Students are promoted to the next grade when they have not mastered the material.

- Aboriginal students complete high school only to find they are not prepared to compete at the postsecondary level.

- No educational requirements are mandatory even for very good jobs. Students actually drop out of school to take excellent jobs.

- Schools hire people for reasons other than merit.

- Qualified Aboriginal workers are not hired because mainstreamers are preferred.

- When mainstream companies are forced by law to hire a percentage of qualified Aboriginal workers, they conform to the law by hiring Aboriginal workers but then tell them to stay away from the job site.

In all these examples, the fundamentals of meritocracy are violated. Even if such violations are infrequent, given that the meritocracy value has not been clearly explained and implemented, mainstream culture appears confusing. Under these circumstances, goals are impossible to formulate, and collective demotivation is the outcome.

Collective Identity and Personal Agency Beliefs

Motivation requires that people believe they are capable of achieving the goal and that the environment provides them with the opportunity to achieve the goal. Instilling such beliefs in a student is difficult enough but is made virtually impossible when there are few models available to demonstrate that it is possible. How can a student come to believe that he or she is capable of reaching a challenging academic goal when, on the one hand, most White Europeans appear to have succeeded, but there are so few Aboriginal role models to draw upon. Such models are crucial, not only because they instill the belief that it is possible, but because they demonstrate in concrete terms *how* it is done.

The importance of role models cannot be overestimated, because it is not sufficient to have only one or two models. Even in the context of European culture, the importance of multiple models arises. For example, as women strived for equality with men in society, more women medical doctors began to emerge. Surprisingly, even women were overheard to claim that they still have more confidence in a male doctor than one who is a woman. Similarly, in Arctic Quebec, when the first trained Inuit pilots took to the sky, many Inuit quietly let it be known that they had more confidence in White pilots than in equally trained Inuit pilots who had the advantage of knowing the land in great detail. Thus, the lack of appropriate models in sufficient numbers means that many lack confidence in their own capability with the result that motivation suffers.

Summary

Most people in the world have a well-defined culture that provides them with a clear set of goals that they can pursue with emotion and confidence.

Moreover, these goals are shared by everyone who was socialized into that culture. Sometimes people are born and raised in one culture, other times they acquire a new culture but only after being exposed to the new culture in all its depth and complexity. The end result is that people are, for the most part, motivated to achieve the cultural goals.

Colonized people, because of their unique circumstances, find themselves suffering from collective demotivation. The two cultures that colonized peoples are exposed to do not enrich their cultural definition, nor is conflict between the two cultures the overriding problem. The problem is that the fundamentals of the heritage culture have been ruptured and only a superficial facsimile of European culture has been offered up. The result is a void in terms of goals or vision, a lack of emotional commitment, and a lack of confidence: in short, collective demotivation.

CHAPTER 8

Toward a Healthy
Collective Identity

On the surface, solution to academic underachievement and the social problems confronting society's most disadvantaged groups seems obvious. I have argued that the root problem is a lack of a coherently defined collective identity and that the pervasive academic underachievement, social dysfunction, and demotivation we are witnessing begin with problems related to collective identity.

Once we scratch the surface, however, it will become apparent that the route to a healthy collective identity will necessitate steps that most would consider odious and contrary to the cherished value that those who are privileged should reach out to the less fortunate. And along the way, it may be necessary to challenge the value of cultural relativism and make responsibility a respectable word.

I have argued that the key characteristics of a healthy collective identity are a clear identity and a widespread commitment to that identity by most, if not all, members of a group. Valueless colonialism and identity overload are, I believe, the two social realities that have dislocated the collective identity of society's most disadvantaged groups. The first, valueless colonialism, refers to a specific power relationship between groups, and the second, identity overload, arises as an unintended consequence of the global explosion in communication and information. Each of these realities needs to be addressed differently, but each impacts the clarity of collective identity.

How, then, can a group carve out a clear collective identity when, because of valueless colonialism and/or identity overload, no such clarity exists? Because collective identity is socially defined, surely all that is needed is for members of a group to recognize that an unclear collective identity is the problem and set about to clarify it. Moreover, articulating a clear collective identity could be the ultimate exercise in democracy because every member of the group contributes to the definition of the group's collective identity. Unfortunately for society's most disadvantaged groups, this democratic ideal is not likely to be realized. What are the chances of every member of a group waking up on the same day and deciding that defining a clear collective identity for the group should be "Job 1" and everyone espousing precisely the same elements central to the new identity? The chances are virtually zero, especially considering the forces that continue to conspire against the articulation of a clear collective identity.

THE GENESIS OF A NEW COLLECTIVE IDENTITY

So who is going to initiate the process of defining a new clearly defined collective identity? Certainly not advantaged colonizing groups. Groups of privilege are not inclined to willingly divest themselves of power or purposely create a new powerful group with whom they might be forced to compete. Furthermore, advantaged colonizing groups have no understanding of, or experience with, having their own collective identity obliterated. While advantaged groups may be sympathetic, they are not in a position to offer disadvantaged groups ready-made solutions for articulating a new collective identity. Certainly the natural forces associated with identity overload will not spontaneously reverse themselves so as to provide a clearly defined collective identity. The inescapable conclusion, then, is that hope for a revitalized, clear collective identity resides with the disadvantaged group itself. More specifically, because the process of collective identity clarification will not be ignited by spontaneous combustion, the responsibility lies squarely on the shoulders of leaders of the disadvantaged group.

Calling for leaders of disadvantaged groups to instigate a genuine redefinition in collective identity is, however, highly problematic. True, group leaders have risen to positions of power and influence and should theoretically be able to effectively mobilize group members toward a redefinition of collective identity; however, their leadership position was attained in the context of the established colonial structure and, hence, group leaders have benefited in part from the very intergroup structure that has led to the dissolution of collective identity. For example, many Aboriginal communities are experiencing, in addition to their social challenges, internal strife around this very issue. Tribal councils, although composed of elected chiefs, nevertheless are accused of not representing their community. Because the very structure of tribal councils is one imposed by mainstream colonizers, elected chiefs are perceived by some as mere puppets of their colonial oppressors. They are "apples," red on the outside but white on the inside. Similarly, some African American leaders are dubbed "oreos" and Hispanic leaders, "coconuts."

But the issue is more complex than questions of perceived leadership legitimacy. Those who have risen to successful positions of leadership are not likely to appreciate the desperate need for change in collective identity because their very success would not make such a need salient. For example, the political leaders in Arctic communities I have worked in are all products of the federal school system, an absolutely draconian process that removed young people from their communities and submerged them in an all-English, colonial environment. Most were abused physically and punished regularly for such transgressions as using their own language. In conversation, these friends would point out that, "However bad such a system was, it worked for me since I am now a so-called acknowledged leader." I would counter by asking them to recall their classmates and list for me their current situations. Eventually they would agree that the number of people who survived the colonial school system to become productive adults was very small, and so today's leaders are extraordinary people who have risen to positions of leadership in spite of, not because of, their colonial experience. Their extraordinary success makes it difficult for them to identify with the collective identity vacuum that pervades the community.

Put very simply, there are severe barriers to the creation of a clear collective identity. First, collective identity is an invisible, psychological construct, and clarity is always more difficult when there is little in the way of concrete elements to serve as a guidepost. Second, successful leaders are uniquely placed to instigate the collective identity process but are least appreciative of the current turmoil associated with identity and have the most to lose should there be changes to collective identity. Finally, the groups who must carve a clear collective identity are those with the least power in a colonial relationship, and there is no obvious mechanism for arresting the problems created by identity overload. Any new identity must be formulated against the backdrop of the very forces that gave rise to problems with collective identity in the first place.

What Would a New Collective Identity Look Like?

Because the group itself must take the initiative in terms of defining a new collective identity, how can we possibly guess what form a group's collective identity will take? The answer is, of course, that we cannot, but having said that, there are certain contextual features that allow us to anticipate some of the elements that will be influential. The elements I am thinking about are destined to create tension in disadvantaged communities as they set about to elaborate a clear collective identity.

Elements of mainstream culture are bound to figure prominently in any disadvantaged group's redefined collective identity. The very cultural power that allowed mainstream culture to obliterate the culture of Aboriginal peoples, African Americans, and certain Hispanic groups will force members of these groups to include elements of mainstream culture in their own collective identity. No group will want to completely dismiss the comforts and advantages that mainstream culture has to offer. Modern technology and key political, judicial, educational, and religious institutions, including the value system they are based on, will be difficult for any group to abandon completely. Arctic communities, for example, are completely dependent on air travel, snowmobiles, and communication technology, and each of these has allowed them to better fulfill their needs in a harsh climate.

Having mainstream culture figure prominently in a redefinition of collective identity is not destructive in and of itself, but the clarity of any redefined collective identity can only be determined in contrast to competing collective identities. That is, a collective identity can only be recognized and understood as such by the manner in which it differs from the collective identity of other groups. Simply put, identity definition is a comparative process. Disadvantaged groups, in their desire to articulate a collective identity, will need to have that identity contrast with other identities. Concretely, this means the need to define a collective identity that differs from mainstream culture, for without such a contrast a group will not have an identity that is definable or unique, let alone clear. But we have already noted that elements of mainstream culture are inescapable. Herein lies the tension: the need for a collective identity that is distinctive, on the one hand, without giving up the elements of mainstream culture that improve the group's quality of life, on the other hand.

Not surprisingly, then, we witness in every disadvantaged community this tension in defining a unique collective identity. In the African American and Hispanic communities, there is the fear of "selling out" to the White community. The result is that more militant propositions for identity gain credibility. The reality is that since the contrast between Martin Luther King and Malcom X, their contrasting views on collective identity have co-existed. And this is true for every disadvantaged group. Among Aboriginal groups, the "warriors" advocate eschewing everything that is mainstream.

These contrasting views within disadvantaged communities have an unexpected outcome on two fronts. On the one hand, mainstream people point to such contrasts as evidence that the group itself does not know what it wants and all they do is fight with one another. However, members of the disadvantaged groups are themselves more comfortable with such contrasting views within their group. They recognize that each competing position represents an aspect of the dilemma each and every one of them feels. Simply put, a collective identity is not carved out in a vacuum but against the backdrop of a volatile history involving mainstream culture whose presence is inescapable.

The Rise of Separatist Movements

Political separatist movements are the clearest example of a people's struggle to define a clear collective identity. There are three separatist movements in North America that most mainstreamers find puzzling. The most formal of these is the so-called separatist movement in Quebec, Canada. The movement is spearheaded by the government in power in Quebec, and the results of a formal referendum held in the fall of 1995 revealed that 49.5 percent of Quebecers voted yes to the political separation of Quebec from the rest of Canada. Why Quebecers might want to separate from what some analysts have judged to be the first-ranked nation in the world in terms of quality of life bewilders most Canadians and, indeed, Americans. The second movement involves Aboriginal people in Canada, both First Nation and Inuit, pressing for land claims and self-government. Finally, while less formal, after decades of pressures toward racial desegregation in the United States, murmurs of racial resegregation are being heard with one enormous difference. It is the African American community that is contemplating the potential gains that might come from institutional separation.

Cynics will describe these separatist movements as the self-centered instigation of those who are merely capitalizing on the structural features that facilitate separation. The most serious of the movements involves a French-speaking minority in Canada and North America but one that has its own formal government, its own language, and its own formal political borders. Aboriginal people do have some degree of self-government and a quasi-formal status to their geographic boundaries, whereas African Americans have no such formal institutional support.

But while geography and political legitimacy may facilitate separation, they in no way guarantee it, and, thus, we are forced to look deeper for any genuine understanding. First, it is instructive that these movements arise among some of the very groups who have suffered the most in terms of threats to their collective identity. The obliteration of Aboriginal and African American collective identity through internal colonialism and slavery have been well documented. The case of French-speaking Quebecers is less obvious, but the parallels are there. Moreover, while the level of oppression experienced by French-speaking Canadians does not approach that of Aboriginal peoples or the descendents of slaves, French-speaking Canadians have more resources. They have a legitimate geographical border and provincial government, a cadre of modern institutions, and a highly skilled professional and technical population. Thus, while their disadvantage may be less than society's most disadvantaged, they have the resources to vigorously address the redefinition of collective identity.

Quebec society has undergone a profound transformation. Although overly simplistic, it has lost many of its key institutions, such as the church and agrarian economy, that were the bedrock of collective identity. These dramatic changes, coupled with French-speaking Quebecers' minority status in North America has left a collective identity vacuum. Perhaps it is not surprising that there would arise a cultural nationalism that is largely secular with a focus on language, culture, and political distinctiveness.

The point here is that all three separatist movements represent precisely what I have been advocating in terms of what is necessary for defining a clear collective identity. Each has taken the responsibility for collective identity upon themselves.

The reaction of mainstream North Americans to these separatist movements is instructive. Advantaged mainstreamers feel threatened on two fronts. First, their position of advantage is threatened and so the predictable reaction is rejection and ridicule. Second, advantaged mainstreamers feel threatened because they are jealous of the passion and allegiance that members of separatist movements have for their collective identity.

Separatist movements, then, most certainly arise in response to perceived injustice, but not all groups that perceive injustice seek political independence through separation. The more usual reaction is a spectrum of pressure tactics designed to redress the perceived injustice. So, while separatist movements rationalize their aim as a response to perceived injustice, there is a less tangible need that leads to separation as a solution. What I am suggesting here is that part of the impetus for such movements is the clearly defined collective identities they provide. Moreover, it is no coincidence that such dramatic movements are spearheaded by society's most disadvantaged groups.

Of Cults, Gangs, and Zero Tolerance

The quest for a clearly defined collective identity is not limited to separatist movements by groups whose collective identity has been systematically destroyed. The confusion in collective identity as a consequence of identity overload, especially among young people, is in evidence everywhere.

In an environment of confusion in collective identity, cults are particularly attractive. They provide for a collective identity that is frighteningly clear and that provides participants with a clearly defined set of long-, medium-, and short-term goals. As well, cults spell out precisely how to achieve those goals. In precisely the same manner, terrorist groups recruit against the backdrop of collective uncertainty about a stable future for their cultural and religious groups.

Gangs serve a similar function for young people. As a society, our response to gangs has been typically self-serving. We focus in on gang members who claim that their gang is a substitute for their family and that it provides them with self-esteem. We then note how most gang members come from broken homes and righteously conclude that if only we could get those dysfunctional families to take responsibility, the problem would be solved. But, of course, the problem is much broader. What is missing is a clearly defined collective identity, an identity whose responsibility lies not merely with the family but with society as a whole. The gang, then, offers members a set of clearly defined goals for the group from which the opportunity for personal identity and esteem derive. In short, like cults, gangs offer a clearly defined collective identity from which all other components of the self flow.

In case we are tempted to dismiss gangs and cults as a problem limited to a few desperate people, an example from mainstream society may be sobering. Isolated schools are beginning to respond with a zero tolerance policy to what, on the surface, are problems with violence and drugs. Contained in such policies are elements of collective identity that are instructive. First, zero tolerance policies arise in a context where educational leaders are frustrated with what everybody agrees is unacceptable behavior. Their response is not to "regulate" the problem but rather to adopt an extreme policy. These policies have been so rigidly implemented that cases have been made public where a 13-year-old student is suspended for bringing to school a tiny knife in his lunch bucket in order to cut his apple. The suspension was immediate, without any inquiry into the motive and circumstances surrounding the incident. On the surface, the suspension appears to be such an overreaction that it provokes public ridicule. Similar incidents involving a young boy kissing a classmate have provoked similar public reactions.

But we need to look deeper into the policies that provoked these overreactions. First, I would argue that they grow out of a much broader desire to articulate a clear collective identity. Education in North America is being besieged with cries of "back to basics." These cries surely reveal society's profound sense that education has lost all sense of purpose, its goals have been clouded. Moreover, in a manner suggestive of identity overload, many are now claiming that schools are being asked to do too much. In addition to basic education, they are asked to baby-sit; teach about sexual problems, safety problems, and harassment problems; and more generally to "street-proof" children.

Thus, it is not surprising that some schools have focused on the most visible of their problems, drugs and violence, the problems about which they are certain to obtain community-wide consensus. And because the desperate need is for clarity, the value or goal must be articulated in the extreme: hence, the need to not merely attempt to improve the situation but, rather, invoke policies of zero tolerance.

Second, these extreme policies revolve around goals that are not likely to provoke much disagreement. Everybody agrees that schools should be drug free and safe. Moreover, they arise in a context where drugs and violence are widespread. Thus, any slippage in implementing a zero tolerance program, be it plastic knife or peck on the cheek, opens the door to a return to the undesirable norm. Flexibility can be desirable against the backdrop of a clear collective identity, not when clarity is being sought and that clarity is the converse of current norms.

Further calls for a return to the three Rs, reading, writing and arithmetic, are more problematic, for here there is not the same community-wide consensus on the goal. But at least it is a goal to fall back on at a time when collective goals are unclear, and, even if there is some disagreement about the details, there is full agreement that the three Rs are important.

For colonized groups, there is no such fallback. In terms of education specifically, there is no cultural history of formal education to use as a template. More generally, in terms of the culture as a whole, colonized groups are forced to fall back on a romanticized image of a bygone era. For African Americans this means looking back to African roots, and for Aboriginal people this means a return to a time prior to European colonizers.

In summary, cults, gangs, and rigid educational policies are, I believe, natural responses to the void that results from people confronting a life, or a domain in their life, that is meaningless. A lack of meaning arises when there are no goals to motivate, and goals require a clear collective identity. And where there is no clear collective identity, there can be no personal identity or esteem.

Despite this summary paragraph, there is some unfinished business that needs to be addressed. How do street kids fit into our discussion of cults and gangs? On the surface, it would be tempting to describe street kids as a form of gang, but unfortunately the fit is not a good one. Gangs are characterized by a clearly defined identity that gang members display proudly. The antiauthority and antiestablishment stance of most gangs is offset by a fierce loyalty to each other and to the group. Moreover, gangs have structure and a clearly defined set of roles with acknowledged leadership. Street kids are striking in that, as much as they are defiant of authority, they appear to have no particular mission, other than to survive, or group structure to satisfy their basic social needs. Thus, street kids do not look to mainstream society for a collective identity, but neither do they have any alternative. Not surprisingly, then, street kids tend to be relatively passive and appear to be directionless. Street gangs seem to have an all too clear collective identity, one that is very much against and therefore a threat to, mainstream collective identity. Therefore, gangs represent a direct threat to society. Street kids are not a threat; they are against mainstream collective identity, but they have no counterpart collective identity and, thus, evoke pity not fear, and they appear unreachable from the perspective of mainstream logic.

So That's Why We Are So Threatened by Social Change

The challenge confronting colonized groups and young mainstreamers today is daunting, but I worry that those of us whose collective identity remains intact can never fully appreciate their plight. Short of "walking a mile in their shoes," we are forced to examine our own experience for any possible examples that may provide us with some appreciation.

The example that comes to mind is the rapidly changing economic and, by extension, social reality that has brought about "downsizing," "rightsizing," "flex hours," "contracting," "job sharing," and work from home. And all of this is exacerbated by the computer revolution that has left most people feeling as if they have been left behind with little chance that they will ever have a conversation with a real human being again. These are rapidly evolving changes that touch all of us, and they underscore how threatening change is for most people. What change does, of course, is leave us, at least temporarily, with no collective identity. Our collective template is disrupted, and until time and social consensus produces an altered collective identity, we lack direction and lose the reference that provides us with personal identity and esteem.

Now let me make it clear that not all changes represent an assault on our collective identity. Most of the changes we confront require adjustment and accommodation but no real need to redefine the fundamentals of our collective identity. Clearly, any change would have to seriously disrupt collective identity before it would be so threatening as to cause widespread dysfunction. Changes in the global economy and information technology are dramatic enough to be very unsettling, but I need to underscore that they do not begin to approach the collective identity vacuum that confronts society's most disadvantaged groups. What is our natural reaction to changes in global communication, the economy, and technology that do unsettle the blueprint provided by our collective identity? It is precisely at such times that we most need our collective identity and, thus, if anything, we look immediately to our existing collective identity and cling to it tenaciously. But, of course, the new reality requires changes to our collective identity. Maladaptively, the greater the required change, the more we seek guidance from our old collective identity, thereby ensuring that our capacity to cope with change is diminished. No wonder we are creatures of habit.

Conclusion

Disadvantaged groups in society are in search of a clearly defined collective identity, but that quest will not evolve smoothly. It is the group itself, spearheaded by group leaders, who must instigate the process. Powerful mainstream groups cannot take it upon themselves to draw up a collective blueprint for others. What advantaged groups can do is respect the need for the process to take place.

In articulating a new collective identity, disadvantaged groups will need to etch the identity with bold strokes. Thus, we can expect that the content of a new collective identity will be extreme and no deviance from that identity will be tolerated from group members.

Finally, since the new collective identity must coexist with the collective identity of powerful mainstream groups, disadvantaged groups will need to be militant in carving a role for their new identity. No one said the process would be easy.

References

Bandura, A. (1977). Self-efficacy: Toward a unifying theory of behavior change. *Psychological Review, 84*, 191–215.

Bandura, A. (1986). Self-regulation of motivation and action through internal standards and goal systems. In L.A. Pervin (Ed.) *Goal concepts in personality and social psychology.* Hillsdale, NJ: Lawrence Erlbaum.

Baumeister, R.F. & Heatherton, T.F. (1996). Self-regulation failure: An overview. *Psychological Inquiry, 7(1)*, 1–15.

Bloom, A. (1987). *The closing of the American mind.* New York: Simon and Shuster.

Cialdini, R.B. (2001). *Influence: Science and practice* (4th ed.). Boston: Allyn and Bacon.

Cocker, M. (1998). *Rivers of blood, rivers of gold: Europe's conquest of indigenous peoples.* New York: Grove Press.

Crago, M.B. & Eriks-Brophy, A. (1993) Feeling right: Approaches to a family's culture. *Volta Review, 95*, 123–129.

Deci, E.L. & Ryan, R.M. (1985). *Intrinsic motivation and self-determination in human behavior.* New York: Plenum

Diamond, J. (1997). *Guns, germs, and steel: The fates of human societies.* New York: W.W. Norton & Company.

Ford, M.E. (1992) *Motivating humans: Goals, emotions, and personal agency beliefs.* Newbury Park, CA: Sage Publications.

Frideres, J.S. (1988). *Native people in Canada: Contemporary conflicts* (3rd Ed.). Scarborough: Prentice-Hall.

Gergen, K.J. (1991). *The saturated self: Dilemmas of identity in contemporary life.* New York: Basic Books Inc.

Hacker, A. (1992). *Two Nations: Black and White, separate, hostile, unequal*. New York: Ballantine Books.

Heath, S.B. (1983). *Ways with words*. Cambridge: Cambridge University Press.

Herrnstein R.J. & Murray, C. (1994). *The bell curve: Intelligence and class structure in American life*. New York: Free Press.

Higgins, E.T. (1987). Self-discrepancy: A theory relating self and affect. *Psychological Review, 94*, 319–340.

Huntington, S.P. (1996). *The clash of civilizations and the remaking of world order*. New York: Touchstone.

Jensen, A.R. (1969). How much can we boost IQ and scholastic achievement? *Harvard Educational Review, 39*, 1–123.

Markus H. & Wurf, E. (1987). The dynamic of self-concept: A social psychological perspective. *Annual Review of Psychology, 38*, 299–337.

Neisser, U., Boodoo, G., Bouchard, T.J., Boykin, A.W., Brody, N., Ceci, S.J., Halpern, D.F., Loehlin, J.C., Perloff, R., Sternberg, R.J. & Urbina, S. (1996). Intelligence: Knowns and unknowns. *American Psychologist, 51*, (2), 77–101.

Ogbu, J.U. & Matute, M.E. (1986). Understanding sociocultural factors: Knowledge, identity, and school adjustment. In *Beyond language: Social and cultural factors in schooling language minority students*. Sacramento: Bilingual Education Office, California State Department of Education.

Publication Manual of the American Psychological Association, 4th ed. 1995.

Rushton, J.P. (1988). Race differences in behavior: A review and evolutionary analysis. *Personality and Individual Differences, 9*, 1009–1024.

Sedekides, C. & Strube M.J. (1995). The multiply motivated self. *Personality and Social Psychology Bulletin, 21*, 1330–1335.

Sowell, T. (1983). *The economics and politics of race: An international perspective*. New York: William Morrow.

Statistics, Canada. (1989). *1986 census of Canada*. The Nation. Population and Dwelling Characteristics. Labour Force Activity. Catalogue no. 93–111. Ottawa: Minister of Regional Industrial Expansion and the Minister of State for Science and Technology.

Statistics, Canada. (1989). *1986 census of Canada*. The Nation. Population and Dwelling Characteristics. Total Income. Catalogue no. 93–114. Ottawa: Minister of Regional Industrial Expansion and the Minister of State for Science and Technology.

Statistics, Canada. (1993). *1991 aboriginal peoples survey*. Schooling, Work and Related Activities, Income, Expenses and Mobility. Catalogue no. 89–534. Ottawa: Minister of Industry, Science and Technology.

Statistics, Canada. *1993 Canadian social trends: School leavers*. Caltalogue no. 11–008E.

Statistics, Canada. *1994 women in the labour force*. Catalogue no. 75–507E. Ottawa: Housing, Family and Social Statistics Division.

Steele, C.M. (1988). The psychology of self-affirmation: Sustaining the integrity of the self. *Advances in Experimental Social-Psychology, 21,* 261–302.

Swann, J.B. Jr. (1990). To be adored or to be known: The interplay of self-enhancement and self-verification. In R.M. Sorrentino and E.T. Higgins (Eds.) *Motivation and cognition,* vol. 2. New York: Guilford Press, pp. 408–448.

Tajfel, H. & Turner, J.C. (1979). An integrative theory of intergroup conflict. In W.G. Austin & S. Worchel (Eds.) *The social psychology of intergroup relations,* Monterey, CA: Brooks/Cole, pp. 33–47.

Tanner, A. (Ed.). (1983). *The politics of Indianness: Case studies of native ethnopolitics in Canada.* St. John's Nfld., Canada: Institute of Social and Economic Research, Memorial University of Newfoundland.

Taylor, C. (1991). *The malaise of modernity.* Concord, Ontario: Anansi.

Turner, J.C. (1987). *Rediscovering the social group: A self-categorization theory.* New York: Basil Blaackwell.

U.S. Census Bureau. (2000). *Statistical abstract of the United States: 2000* (120th edition). Washington, DC.

Wicklund, R.A. & Gollwitzer, P.M. (1982). *Symbolic self-completion.* Hillsdale, NJ: Erlbaum.

Wright, S.C., Taylor, D.M. & Ruggiero, K.M. (1996). Examining the potential for academic achievement among Inuit children: Comparisons on the raven colored progressive matrices. *Journal of Cross-Cultural Psychology, 27, 6,* 733–753.

Index

About the Author

DONALD M. TAYLOR is Professor of Psychology at McGill University. His previous publications include *Coping with Cultural and Racial Diversity* (Praeger, 1990) and *Theories of Intergroup Relations, 2nd editon* (Praeger, 1994).